Lenin and Philosophy
and other Essays

LENIN AND PHILOSOPHY
AND OTHER ESSAYS

Louis Althusser

TRANSLATED FROM THE FRENCH
BY BEN BREWSTER

Monthly Review Press
New York and London

Foreword

I am glad to be able to extend a few words of welcome to the reader who does me the honour of opening this book.

I trust him: he will understand the political, ideological and theoretical arguments which inspired the already old philosophical essays in the Appendix; he will discern in them an internal evolution and displacement giving rise to the new Theses which appear in 'Lenin and Philosophy', 'Preface to *Capital* Volume One' and 'Ideology and Ideological State Apparatuses'; he will realize that it is in the direction opened by the indications in these last texts that I now feel it necessary to pursue an investigation which I began more than fifteen years ago.

If I wished to sum up the peculiar object and ambitions of this investigation in a few words, I should say, *first*, that at a time and in a world which either stubbornly fight against Marx or cover him in academic honours while distorting him in bourgeois interpretations (economism, technocratism, humanism), I have tried to re-emphasize the fact that we owe to him the greatest discovery of human history: the discovery that opens for men the way to a *scientific* (materialist and dialectical) understanding of their own history as a history of the class struggle.

I should *then* say that this science cannot be a science like any other, a science for 'everyone'. Precisely because it reveals the mechanisms of class exploitation, repression and domination, in the economy, in politics and in ideology, it cannot be recognized by *everyone*. This science, which brings the social classes face to face with their truth, is unbearable for the bourgeoisie and its allies, who reject it and take refuge in their so-called 'social sciences': it is only acceptable to the proletariat, whom it 'represents' (Marx). That is why the proletariat has recognized it as its own property, and has set it to work in its practice: in the hands of the Workers' Movement, Marxist science has become the theoretical weapon of the revolution.

I should say, *lastly*, that *class conditions in theory* had to be achieved for Marx to be able to conceive and carry out his *scientific* work. So long as he remained on bourgeois and petty-bourgeois positions, Marx was still subject to the ruling ideology, whose function it is to mask the mechanisms of class exploitation. But it is only from the point of view of class exploitation that it is possible to *see* and analyse the mechanisms of a class society and therefore to produce a scientific knowledge of it. The story of Marx's Early Works and his rupture with his 'erstwhile philosophical consciousness' prove this: in order to fulfil the conditions that govern the science of history, Marx had to abandon his bourgeois and then petty-bourgeois class positions and adopt the class positions of the proletariat. That these class conditions are not 'given' in advance, that all Marx's work contributed to their elaboration, makes no difference to this principle: it is only from the point of view of the exploited class that it is possible to discover, against all bourgeois ideology and even against classical Political Economy, the mechanisms of those relations of exploitation, the relations of production of a class society.

When one reads Marx's works, this *change of position* takes the form of a *'critique'*: a constant critique, from the Early

Works to *Capital* (subtitled 'A *Critique* of Political Economy'). One might therefore think that it was a matter of
a purely intellectual development. Certainly, Marx's extraordinary critical intelligence is at work in this development.
But on Marx's own admission, it is the theoretical effect of
a determinant cause: the struggle of the contemporary
classes, and above all, since they gave it its meaning, the
first forms of the class struggle (before 1848) and then the
great class struggles *of the proletariat* (1848–49; 1871). That
political class struggle can have radical effects in theory, this
we know: the political class struggle resounds in the ideological and philosophical class struggle; it can therefore
succeed in transforming class positions in theory. Without
the proletariat's class struggle, Marx could not have adopted
the point of view of class exploitation, or carried out his
scientific work. In this scientific work, which bears the mark
of all his culture and genius, he has given back to the
Workers' Movement in a theoretical form what he took
from it in a political and ideological form.

I close on this comment because it is vital for us, who live
one hundred years after *Capital*. Marx's work, although
completely scientific, is not something gained which is sec-
urely available to us. In order to defend Marx's work, in
order to develop and apply it, we are subject to the same
class conditions in theory. It is only on the positions of the
proletariat that it is possible to provide a radical critique of
the new forms of bourgeois ideology, to obtain thereby a
clear view of the mechanisms of imperialism and to advance
in the construction of socialism. The struggle for Marxist
science and Marxist philosophy is today, as it was yesterday,
a form of political and ideological class struggle. This
struggle entails a radical critique of all forms of bourgeois
ideology and of all 'bourgeois' interpretations of Marxism.
At the same time, it demands the maximum attention to the

resources, new forms and *inventions* of the class struggle of the proletariat and of the oppressed peoples of the world.

In a time like ours, dominated by the split in the International Communist Movement, we still need to meditate this lesson of Marx's: of this man for whom the proletarian revolutions of 1848 had opened the way to science, this man who attended the school of the Commune in order to be able to map out the future of socialism.

Louis Althusser
Paris, June 1970

Philosophy as a Revolutionary Weapon

Interview conducted by
Maria Antonietta Macciocchi

I

Can you tell us a little about your personal history? What brought you to Marxist philosophy?

In 1948, when I was 30, I became a teacher of philosophy and joined the PCF. Philosophy was an interest; I was trying to make it my profession. Politics was a passion; I was trying to become a Communist militant.

My interest in philosophy was aroused by materialism and its critical function: for *scientific* knowedge, against all the mystifications of *ideological* 'knowledge'. Against the merely moral denunciation of myths and lies, for their rational and rigorous criticism. My passion for politics was inspired by the revolutionary instinct, intelligence, courage and heroism of the working class in its struggle for socialism. The War and the long years of captivity had brought me into living contact with workers and peasants, and acquainted me with Communist militants.

It was politics which decided everything. Not politics in general: Marxist-Leninist politics.

First I had to find them and understand them. That is always extremely difficult for an intellectual. It was just as difficult in the fifties and sixties, for reasons with which you are familiar: the consequences of the 'cult', the Twentieth Congress, then the crisis of the international Communist

Movement. Above all, it was not easy to resist the spread of contemporary 'humanist' ideology, and bourgeois ideology's other assaults on Marxism.

Once I had a better understanding of Marxist-Leninist politics, I began to have a passion for philosophy *too*, for at last I began to understand the great thesis of Marx, Lenin and Gramsci: that philosophy is fundamentally *political*.

Everything that I have written, at first alone, later in collaboration with younger comrades and friends, revolves, despite the 'abstraction' of our essays, around these very concrete questions.

2

Can you be more precise: why is it generally so difficult to be a Communist in philosophy?

To be a Communist in philosophy is to become a partisan and artisan of Marxist-Leninist philosophy: of dialectical materialism.

It is not easy to become a Marxist-Leninist philosopher. Like every 'intellectual', a philosophy teacher is a petty bourgeois. When he opens his mouth, it is petty-bourgeois ideology that speaks: its resources and ruses are infinite.

You know what Lenin says about 'intellectuals'. Individually certain of them may (politically) be declared *revolutionaries*, and courageous ones. But as a mass, they remain 'incorrigibly' petty-bourgeois in ideology. Gorky himself was, for Lenin, who admired his talents, a *petty-bourgeois* revolutionary. To become 'ideologists of the working class' (Lenin), 'organic intellectuals' of the proletariat (Gramsci), intellectuals have to carry out a radical revolution in their ideas: a long, painful and difficult re-education. An endless external and *internal* struggle.

Proletarians have a 'class instinct' which helps them on

the way to proletarian 'class positions'. Intellectuals, on the contrary, have a petty-bourgeois class instinct which fiercely resists this transition.

A proletarian *class position* is more than a mere proletarian 'class instinct'. It is the consciousness and practice which conform with the *objective* reality of the proletarian class struggle. Class instinct is subjective and spontaneous. Class position is objective and rational. To arrive at proletarian class positions, the class instinct of proletarians only needs to be *educated*; the class instinct of the petty bourgeoisie, and hence of intellectuals, has, on the contrary, to be *revolutionized*. This education and this revolution are, in the last analysis, determined by proletarian class struggle conducted on the basis of the principles of Marxist-Leninist *theory*.

As the *Communist Manifesto* says, knowledge of this *theory* can help *certain* intellectuals to go over to working-class positions.

Marxist-Leninist theory includes a *science* (historical materialism) and a *philosophy* (dialectical materialism).

Marxist-Leninist philosophy is therefore one of the two *theoretical* weapons indispensable to the class struggle of the proletariat. Communist militants must assimilate and use the principles of the theory: science and philosophy. The proletarian revolution needs militants who are both scientists (historical materialism) and philosophers (dialectical materialism) to assist in the defence and development of theory.

The formation of these philosophers runs up against two great difficulties.

A first – *political* – difficulty. A professional philosopher who joins the Party remains, ideologically, a petty bourgeois. He must revolutionize his thought in order to occupy a proletarian class position in philosophy.

This political difficulty is '*determinant* in the last instance'.

A second – *theoretical* – difficulty. We know in what direction and with what principles we must work in order to define this class position in *philosophy*. But we must develop Marxist philosophy: it is theoretically and politically urgent to do so. Now, this work is vast and difficult. For in Marxist theory, philosophy has lagged behind the science of history.

Today, in our countries, this is the '*dominant*' difficulty.

3

You therefore distinguish between a science and a philosophy in Marxist theory? As you know, this distinction is often contested today.

I know. But this 'contestation' is an old story.

To be *extremely* schematic, it may be said that, in the history of the Marxist movement, the suppression of this distinction has expressed either a rightist or a leftist deviation. The rightist deviation suppresses philosophy: only science is left (positivism). The leftist deviation suppresses science: only philosophy is left (subjectivism). There are 'exceptions' to this (cases of 'inversion'), but they 'confirm' the rule.

The great leaders of the Marxist Workers' Movement from Marx and Engels to today have always said: these deviations are the result of the influence and domination of bourgeois ideology over Marxism. For their part, they always defended the distinction (science, philosophy), not only for theoretical, *but also* for vital political reasons. Think of Lenin in *Materialism and Empirio-criticism* or '*Left-Wing*' *Communism*. His reasons are blindingly obvious.

4

How do you justify this distinction between science and philosophy in Marxist theory?

I shall answer you by formulating a number of provisional and schematic theses.

1. The fusion of Marxist theory and the Workers' Movement is the most important event in the whole history of the class struggle, i.e. in practically the whole of human *history* (first effects: the socialist revolutions).

2. Marxist theory (science and philosophy) represents an unprecedented revolution in the history of human knowledge.

3. Marx founded a new science: the science of history. Let me use an image. The sciences we are familiar with have been installed in a number of great 'continents'. Before Marx, two such continents had been opened up to scientific knowledge: the continent of Mathematics and the continent of Physics. The first by the Greeks (Thales), the second by Galileo. Marx opened up a third continent to scientific knowledge: the continent of History.

4. The opening up of this new continent has induced a revolution in philosophy. That is a law: philosophy is always linked to the sciences.

Philosophy was born (with Plato) at the opening up of the continent of Mathematics. It was transformed (with Descartes) by the opening up of the continent of Physics. Today it is being revolutionized by the opening up of the continent of History by Marx. This revolution is called dialectical materialism.

Transformations of philosophy are always rebounds from great scientific discoveries. Hence *in essentials*, they arise *after the event*. That is why philosophy has lagged behind science in Marxist theory. There are other reasons which we all know about. But at present this is the dominant one.

5. As a mass, only proletarian militants have recognized the revolutionary scope of Marx's scientific discovery. Their political practice has been transformed by it.

And here we come to the greatest *theoretical* scandal in contemporary history.

As a mass, the intellectuals, on the contrary, even those whose 'professional' concern it is (specialists in the human sciences, philosophers), have not really recognized, or have refused to recognize, the unprecedented scope of Marx's scientific discovery, which they have condemned and despised, and which they distort when they do discuss it.

With a few exceptions, they are still 'dabbling' in political economy, sociology, ethnology, 'anthropology', 'social psychology', etc., etc. . . ., even today, *one hundred years after Capital*, just as some *Aristotelian* physicists were still 'dabbling' in physics, *fifty years after* Galileo. Their 'theories' are ideological anachronisms, rejuvenated with a large dose of intellectual subtleties and ultra-modern mathematical techniques.

But this theoretical scandal is not a scandal at all. It is an effect of the ideological class struggle: for it is bourgeois ideology, bourgeois 'culture' which is in power, which exercises 'hegemony'. As a mass, the intellectuals, including many Communist and Marxist intellectuals, are, *with exceptions*, dominated in their theories by bourgeois ideology. *With exceptions*, the same thing happens in the 'human' sciences.

6. The same scandalous situation in philosophy. Who has understood the astounding philosophical revolution induced by Marx's discovery? Only proletarian militants and leaders. As a mass, on the contrary, professional philosophers have not even suspected it. When they mention Marx it is always, with extremely rare exceptions, to attack

him, to condemn him, to 'absorb' him, to exploit him or to *revise* him.

Those, like Engels and Lenin, who have defended dialectical materialism, are treated as philosophically insignificant. The real scandal is that certain Marxist philosophers have succumbed to the same infection, in the name of 'anti-dogmatism'. But here, too, the reason is the same: the effect of the ideological class struggle. For it is bourgeois ideology, bourgeois 'culture', which is in power.

7. The crucial tasks of the Communist movement *in theory*:
– to recognize and know the revolutionary theoretical scope of Marxist-Leninist science and philosophy;
– to struggle against the bourgeois and petty-bourgeois world outlook which always threatens Marxist theory, and which deeply impregnates it today. The *general* form of this world outlook: *Economism* (today 'technocracy') and its 'spiritual complement' *Ethical Idealism* (today 'Humanism'). Economism and Ethical Idealism have constituted the basic opposition in the bourgeois world outlook since the origins of the bourgeoisie. The current *philosophical* form of this world outlook: *neo-positivism* and its 'spiritual complement', existentialist-phenomenological subjectivism. The variant *peculiar* to the Human Sciences: the *ideology* called 'structuralist';
– to conquer for science the majority of the Human Sciences, above all, the Social Sciences, which, with exceptions, have occupied as imposters the continent of History, the continent whose keys Marx has given us;
– to develop the new science and philosophy with all the necessary rigour and daring, linking them to the requirements and inventions of the practice of revolutionary class struggle.

In *theory*, the decisive link at present: Marxist-Leninist philosophy.

5

*You have said two apparently contradictory or different things:
1. philosophy is basically political; 2. philosophy is linked to
the sciences. How do you conceive this double relationship?*

Here again I shall give my answer in the form of schematic
and provisional theses.

1. The class positions in confrontation in the class
struggle are *'represented'* in the domain of practical ideologies
(religious, ethical, legal, political, aesthetic ideologies) by
world outlooks of antagonistic tendencies: in the last instance
idealist (bourgeois) and materialist (proletarian). Everyone
had a world outlook spontaneously.

2. World outlooks are *represented* in the domain of *theory*
(science + the 'theoretical' ideologies which surround
science and scientists) by *philosophy*. Philosophy represents
the class struggle in theory. That is why philosophy is a
struggle (*Kampf*, said Kant), and basically a *political*
struggle: a class struggle. Everyone is not a philosopher
spontaneously, but everyone may become one.

3. Philosophy exists as soon as the theoretical *domain*
exists: as soon as a *science* (in the strict sense) exists. Without
sciences, no philosophy, only world outlooks. The *stake* in
the battle and the battle-*field* must be distinguished. The
ultimate stake of philosophical struggle is the struggle *for
hegemony* between the two great tendencies in world outlook
(materialist and idealist). The *main* battlefield in this
struggle is scientific knowledge: for it or against it. The
number-one philosophical battle therefore takes place on
the frontier between the scientific and the ideological. There
the idealist philosophies which exploit the sciences struggle
against the materialist philosophies which serve the sciences.
The philosophical struggle is a sector of the class struggle
between world outlooks. In the past, materialism has always
been *dominated* by idealism.

4. The science founded by Marx has changed the whole situation in the theoretical domain. It is a *new* science: the science of history. Therefore, for the first time ever, it has enabled us to know the world outlooks which philosophy represents in theory; it enables us to know philosophy. It provides the means to transform the world outlooks (revolutionary class struggle conducted according to the principles of Marxist theory). Philosophy is therefore doubly revolutionized. Mechanistic materialism, 'idealistic in history', becomes dialectical materialism. The balance of forces is reversed: now materialism can dominate idealism in philosophy, and, if the political conditions are realized, it can carry the class struggle for hegemony between world outlooks.

Marxist-Leninist philosophy, or dialectical materialism, represents the proletarian class struggle *in theory*. In the union of Marxist theory and the Workers' Movement (the *ultimate* reality of the union of theory and practice) philosophy ceases, as Marx said, to 'interpret the world'. It becomes a weapon with which 'to change it': *revolution*.

6

Are these the reasons which have made you say that it is essential to read Capital *today?*

Yes. It is essential to read and study *Capital*.

– in order really to understand, in all its scope and all its scientific and philosophical consequences, what proletarian militants have long understood in practice: the revolutionary character of Marxist theory.

– in order to defend that theory against all the bourgeois and petty-bourgeois interpretations, i.e. revisions, which seriously threaten it today: in the first place the opposition Economism/Humanism.

– in order to develop Marxist theory and produce the scientific concepts indispensable to the analysis of the class struggle today, in our countries and elsewhere.

It is essential to read and study *Capital*. I should add, it is necessary, essential to read and study Lenin, and all the great texts, old and new, to which has been consigned the experience of the class struggle of the international Workers' Movement. It is essential to study the practical works of the Revolutionary Workers' Movement in their reality, their problems and their contradictions: their past and, above all, their *present* history.

In our countries there are immense resources for the revolutionary class struggle today. But they must be sought where they are: in the exploited masses. They will not be 'discovered' without close contact with the masses, and without the weapons of Marxist-Leninist theory. The bourgeois ideological notions of 'industrial society', 'neo-capitalism', 'new working class', 'affluent society', 'alienation' and *tutti quanti* are anti-scientific and anti-Marxist: built to fight revolutionaries.

I should therefore add one further remark: the most important of all.

In order really to understand what one 'reads' and studies in these theoretical, political and historical works, one must directly experience oneself the two *realities* which determine them through and through: the reality of theoretical practice (science, philosophy) in its concrete life; the reality of the *practice of revolutionary class struggle* in its concrete life, in close contact with the masses. For if theory enables us to understand the laws of history, it is not intellectuals, nor even theoreticians, it is the *masses* who make history. It is essential to learn with theory – but at the same time and crucially, it is essential to learn with the masses.

7

You attach a great deal of importance to rigour, including a rigorous vocabulary. Why is that?

A single word sums up the *master* function of philosophical practice: '*to draw a dividing line*' between the true ideas and false ideas. Lenin's words.

But the same word sums up one of the essential operations in the direction of the practice of class struggle: '*to draw a dividing line*' between the antagonistic classes. Between our class friends and our class enemies.

It is the same word. A theoretical dividing line between true ideas and false ideas. A political dividing line between the people (the proletariat and its allies) and the people's enemies.

Philosophy represents the people's class struggle in theory. In return it helps the people to distinguish in *theory* and in all *ideas* (political, ethical, aesthetic, etc.) between true ideas and false ideas. In principle, true ideas always serve the people; false ideas always serve the enemies of the people.

Why does philosophy fight over words? The realities of the class struggle are 'represented' by 'ideas' which are 'represented' by words. In scientific and philosophical reasoning, the words (concepts, categories) are 'instruments' of knowledge. But in political, ideological and philosophical struggle, the words are also weapons, explosives or tranquillizers and poisons. Occasionally, the whole class struggle may be summed up in the struggle for one word against another word. Certain words struggle amongst themselves as enemies. Other words are the site of an *ambiguity*: the stake in a decisive but undecided battle.

For example: Communists struggle for the suppression

of *classes* and for a communist society, where, one day, all men will be free and brothers. However, the whole classical Marxist tradition has refused to say that Marxism is a *Humanism*. Why? Because *practically*, i.e. in *the facts*, the word Humanism is exploited by an ideology which uses it to fight, i.e. to kill, another, true, word, and one vital to the proletariat: the *class struggle*.

For example : revolutionaries know that, *in the last instance*, everything depends not on techniques, weapons, etc., but on militants, on their class consciousness, their devotion and their courage. However, the whole Marxist tradition has refused to say that it is '*man*' who makes history. Why? Because practically, i.e. in *the facts*, this expression is exploited by bourgeois ideology which uses it to fight, i.e. to kill another, true, expression, one vital for the proletariat: *it is the masses who make history*.

At the same time, philosophy, even in the lengthy works where it is most abstract and difficult, fights over words: against lying words, against ambiguous words; for correct words. It fights over 'shades of opinion'.

Lenin said: 'Only short-sighted people can consider factional disputes and a strict differentiation between shades of opinion inopportune or superfluous. The fate of Russian Social-Democracy for very many years to come may depend on the strengthening of one or the other "shade".' (*What is to be Done?*).

The philosophical fight over words is a part of the political fight. Marxist-Leninist philosophy can only complete its abstract, rigorous and systematic theoretical work on condition that it fights both about very 'scholarly' words (concept, theory, dialectic, alienation, etc.) and about very simple words (man, masses, people, class struggle).

February 1968

Lenin and Philosophy

May I thank your Society for the honour it has done me in
inviting me to present to it what it has called, since it came
into existence, and what it will doubtless long continue
to call, by a disarmingly nostalgic name: a communication.[1]

I

A scientist is justified in presenting a communication before
a scientific society. A communication and a discussion are
only possible if they are *scientific*. But a philosophical communication and a philosophical discussion?

Philosophical communication. This term would certainly
have made Lenin laugh, with that whole-hearted, open
laugh by which the fishermen of Capri recognized him as
one of their kind and on their side. This was exactly sixty
years ago, in 1908. Lenin was then at Capri, as a guest
of Gorky, whose generosity he liked and whose talent he
admired, but whom he treated nevertheless as a petty-
bourgeois revolutionary. Gorky had invited him to Capri to

1. A communication presented to the Société Française de Philosophie on
24 February 1968 and reproduced with the permission of its president,
M. Jean Wahl.

take part in philosophical discussions with a small group of Bolshevik intellectuals whose positions Gorky shared, the *Otzovists*. 1908: the aftermath of the first October Revolution, that of 1905, the ebb-tide and repression of the Workers' Movement. And also disarray among the 'intellectuals', including the Bolshevik intellectuals. Several of them had formed a group known to history by the name *'Otzovists'*.

Politically, the Otzovists were leftists, in favour of radical measures: recall (*otzovat'*) of the Party's Duma Representatives, rejection of every form of legal action and immediate recourse to violent action. But these leftist proclamations concealed rightist *theoretical* positions. The Otzovists were infatuated with a fashionable philosophy or philosophical fashion, 'empirio-criticism', which had been updated in form by the famous Austrian physicist, Ernst Mach. This physicists' and physiologists' philosophy (Mach was not just anybody: he has left his name in the history of the sciences) was not without affinity with other philosophies manufactured by scientists like Henri Poincaré, and by historians of science like Pierre Duhem and Abel Rey.

These are phenomena which we are beginning to understand. When certain sciences undergo important revolutions (at that time Mathematics and Physics), there will always be professional *philosophers* to proclaim that the 'crisis in science', or mathematics, or physics, has begun. These philosophers' proclamations are, if I may say so, normal: for a whole category of philosophers spend their time predicting, i.e. awaiting, the last gasp of the sciences, in order to administer them the last rites of philosophy, *ad majorem gloriam Dei*.

But what is more curious is the fact that, at the same time, there will be *scientists* who talk of a crisis in the sciences, and suddenly discover a surprising philosophical vocation – in

which they see themselves as suddenly converted into philosophers, although in fact they were always 'practising'
philosophy – in which they believe they are uttering revela-
tions, although in fact they are merely repeating platitudes
and anachronisms which come from what philosophy is
obliged to regard as its history.

We are philosophers by trade, so we are inclined to think
that if there is a 'crisis', it is a visible and spectacular
philosophical crisis into which these scientists have worked
themselves up when faced with the growth of a science
which they have taken for its conversion, just as a child can
be said to have worked itself up into a feverish crisis. Their
spontaneous, everyday philosophy has simply become *visible
to them*.

Mach's empirio-criticism, and all its by-products, the
philosophies of Bogdanov, Lunacharsky, Bazarov, etc., represented a philosophical crisis of this kind. Such crises are
chronic occurrences. To give some contemporary idea of
this, other things being equal, we can say that the philosophy
which certain biologists, geneticists and linguists today are
busy manufacturing around 'information theory' is a little
philosophical 'crisis' of the same kind, in this case a
euphoric one.

Now what is remarkable about these scientists' philosophical crises is the fact that they are always orientated
philosophically in one and the same direction: they revive
and update old *empiricist* or *formalist*, i.e. *idealist* themes;
they are therefore *always* directed against *materialism*.

So the Otzovists were empirio-criticists, but since (as
Bolsheviks) they were Marxists, they said that Marxism
had to rid itself of that pre-critical metaphysics, 'dialectical
materialism', and that in order to become the Marxism of
the twentieth century, it had at last to furnish itself with
the philosophy it had always lacked, precisely this vaguely

neo-Kantian idealist philosophy, remodelled and authenticated by scientists: *empirio-criticism*. Some Bolsheviks of this group even wanted to integrate into Marxism the 'authentic' humane values of religion, and to this end called themselves 'God-builders'. But we can ignore this.

So Gorky's aim was to invite Lenin to discuss philosophy with the group of Otzovist philosophers. Lenin laid down his conditions: Dear Alexei Maximovich, I should very much like to see you, but I refuse to engage in *any philosophical discussion*.

To be sure, this was a tactical attitude: since political unity among the Bolshevik émigrés was essential, they should not be divided by a philosophical dispute. But we can discern in this tactic much more than a tactic, something I should like to call a *'practice'* of philosophy, and the consciousness of what practising philosophy means; in short the consciousness of the ruthless, primary fact that philosophy *divides*. If science unites, and if it unites without dividing, philosophy divides, and it can only unite by dividing. We can thus understand Lenin's laughter: there is no such thing as philosophical communication, no such thing as philosophical discussion.

All I want to do today is to comment on that laughter, which is a thesis in itself.

I venture to hope that this thesis will lead us somewhere.

And it leads me straightaway to ask myself the question which others cannot fail to ask: if no philosophical communication is possible, then what kind of talk can I give here? It is obviously a talk to philosophers. But as clothes do not make the man, the audience does not make a talk. My talk will therefore not be philosophical.

Nevertheless, for necessary reasons linked to the point we have reached in theoretical history, it will be a talk *in* philosophy. But this talk in philosophy will not quite be a talk *of* philosophy. It will be, or rather will try to be, a talk *on* philosophy. Which means that by inviting me to present a *communication*, your Society has anticipated my wishes.

What I should like to say will indeed deserve that title if, as I hope, I can communicate to you something *on* philosophy, in short, some rudimentary elements towards the idea of a *theory* of philosophy. Theory: something which in a certain way anticipates a science.

That is how I ask you to understand my title: Lenin *and* Philosophy. Not Lenin's philosophy, but Lenin *on* philosophy. In fact, I believe that what we owe to Lenin, something which is perhaps not completely unprecedented, but certainly invaluable, is the beginnings of the ability to talk a kind of discourse which anticipates what will one day perhaps be a non-philosophical theory of philosophy.

2

If such is really Lenin's greatest merit with respect to our present concern, we can perhaps begin by quickly settling an old, open dispute between academic philosophy, including French academic philosophy, and Lenin. As I too am an academic and teach philosophy. I am among those who should wear Lenin's 'cap', if it fits.

To my knowledge, with the exception of Henri Lefebvre who has devoted an excellent little book to him, French academic philosophy has not deigned to concern itself with the man who led the greatest political revolution in modern history and who, in addition, made a lengthy and conscientious analysis in *Materialism and Empirio-criticism* of the works of our compatriots Henri Poincaré, Pierre Duhem and Abel Rey, not to speak of others.

I hope that any of our luminaries whom I have forgotten will forgive me, but it seems to me that, if we except articles by Communist philosophers and scientists, I can hardly find more than a few pages devoted to Lenin in the last half-century: by Sartre in *Les Temps Modernes* in 1946 ('Matérialisme et Révolution'), by Merleau-Ponty (in *Les Aventures de la Dialectique*) and by Ricœur (in an article in *Esprit*).

In the last named, Ricœur speaks of *State and Revolution* with respect, but he does not seem to deal with Lenin's 'philosophy'. Sartre says that the materialist philosophy of Engels and Lenin is 'unthinkable' in the sense of an *Unding*, a thought which cannot stand the test of mere thought, since it is a naturalistic, pre-critical, pre-Kantian and pre-Hegelian metaphysic; but he generously concedes that it may have the function of a Platonic 'myth' which helps proletarians to be revolutionaries. Merleau-Ponty dismisses it with a single word: Lenin's philosophy is an 'expedient'.

It would surely be unbecoming on my part, even given all the requisite tact, to open a case against the French philosophical tradition of the last one hundred and fifty years, since the silence in which French philosophy has *buried* this past is worth more than any *open* indictment. It must really be a tradition which hardly bears looking at, for to this day no prominent French philosopher has dared publicly to write its history.

Indeed, it takes some courage to admit that French philosophy, from Maine de Biran and Cousin to Bergson and Brunschvicg, by way of Ravaisson, Hamelin, Lachelier and Boutroux, can only be *salvaged* from its own history by the few great minds against whom it set its face, like Comte and Durkheim, or buried in oblivion, like Cournot and Couturat; by a few conscientious historians of philosophy, historians of science and epistemologists who worked patiently and silently to educate those to whom in part French philosophy owes its renaissance in the last thirty years. We all know these names; forgive me if I only cite those who are no longer with us: Cavaillès and Bachelard.[2]

After all, this French academic philosophy, profoundly religious, spiritualist and reactionary one hundred and fifty years ago, then in the best of cases conservative, finally belatedly liberal and 'personalist', this philosophy which magnificently ignored Hegel, Marx and Freud, this academic philosophy which only seriously began to read Kant, then Hegel and Husserl, and even to discover the existence of Frege and Russell a few decades ago, and sometimes less, why should it have concerned itself with this Bolshevik, revolutionary, and politician, Lenin?

Besides the overwhelming class pressures on its strictly philosophical traditions, besides the condemnation by its most 'liberal' spirits of 'Lenin's unthinkable pre-critical philosophical thought', the French philosophy which we have inherited has lived in the conviction that it can have nothing philosophical to learn either from a politician or from politics. To give just one example, it was only a little while ago that a few French academic philosophers first turned to the study of the great theoreticians of political philosophy, Machiavelli, Spinoza, Hobbes, Grotius, Locke and even Rousseau, 'our' Rousseau. Only thirty years earlier, these authors were abandoned to literary critics and jurists as left-overs.

But French academic philosophy was not mistaken in its radical refusal to learn anything from politicians and politics, and therefore from Lenin. Everything which touches

2. Now, alas, we have to add the name of Jean Hyppolite to this list.

on politics may be fatal to philosophy, for philosophy lives on politics.

Of course, it cannot be said that, if academic philosophy has ever read him, Lenin did not more than repay it in kind, 'leaving it the change'! Listen to him in *Materialism and Empirio-criticism*, invoking Dietzgen, the German proletarian who Marx and Engels said had discovered '*dialectical materialism*' 'all by himself', as an auto-didact, because he was a proletarian militant:

'*Graduated flunkeys*', who with their talk of '*ideal blessings*' stultify the people by their tortuous '*idealism*' – that is J. Dietzgen's opinion of the professors of philosophy. '*Just as the antipodes of the good God is the devil, so the professorial priest had his opposite pole in the materialist.*' The materialist theory of knowledge is '*a universal weapon against religious belief*', and not only against the '*notorious, formal and common religion of the priests, but also against the most refined, elevated professorial religion of muddled idealists*'. Dietzgen was ready to prefer '*religious honesty*' to the '*half-heartedness*' of free-thinking professors, for '*there a system prevails*', there we find integral people, people who do not separate theory from practice. For the Herr Professors '*philosophy is not a science, but a means of defence against Social-Democracy*'. '*Those who call themselves philosophers – professors and university lecturers – are, despite their apparent free-thinking, more or less immersed in superstition and mysticism . . . and in relation to Social-Democracy constitute a single . . . reactionary mass.*' '*Now, in order to follow the true path, without being led astray by all the religious and philosophical gibberish, it is necessary to study the falsest of all false paths (der Holzweg der Holzwege), philosophy*' (*Materialism and Empirio-criticism, Collected Works*, Moscow, 1962, Vol. 14, pp. 340–41).[3]

Ruthless though it is, this text also manages to distinguish between 'free-thinkers' and 'integral people', even when they are *religious*, who have a 'system' which is not just speculative but inscribed in their practice. It is also lucid:

3. I have italicized Lenin's quotations from Dietzgen. Lenin himself stressed the key phrase '*der Holzweg der Holzwege*'.

it is no accident that it ends with an astonishing phrase of Dietzgen's, which Lenin quotes: we need to follow a true path; but in order to follow a true path it is necessary to *study* philosophy, which is *'the falsest of all false paths'* (der Holzweg der Holzwege). Which means, to speak plainly, that there can be no true path (*sc.* in the sciences, but above all in politics) without a study, and, eventually a *theory of philosophy as a false path*.

In the last resort, and more important than all the reasons I have just evoked, this is undoubtedly why Lenin is *intolerable* to academic philosophy, and, to avoid hurting anyone, to the vast majority of philosophers, if not to all philosophers, whether academic or otherwise. He is, or has been on one occasion or another, philosophically intolerable to everyone (and obviously I also mean myself). Intolerable, basically, because despite all they may say about the pre-critical character of his philosophy and the summary aspect of some of his categories, philosophers feel and know that this is not *the* real question. They feel and know that Lenin is profoundly indifferent to their objections. He is indifferent first, because he foresaw them long ago. Lenin said himself: I am not a philosopher, I am badly prepared in this domain (Letter to Gorky, 7 February 1908). Lenin said: I know that my formulations and definitions are vague, unpolished; I know that philosophers are going to accuse my materialism of being 'metaphysical'. But he adds: that is not the question. Not only do I not 'philosophize' with their philosophy, I do not 'philosophize' like them at all. Their way of 'philosophizing' is to expend fortunes of intelligence and subtlety for no other purpose than to *ruminate in* philosophy. Whereas I treat philosophy differently, I *practise* it, as Marx intended, in obedience to what it is. That is why I believe I am a 'dialectical materialist'.

Materialism and Empirio-criticism contains all this, either directly or between the lines. And that is why Lenin the philosopher is intolerable to most philosophers, who do not want to know, i.e. who realize without admitting it, that this is *the real question*. The real question is not whether Marx, Engels and Lenin are or are not real philosophers, whether their philosophical statements are formally irreproachable, whether they do or do not make foolish statements about Kant's 'thing-in-itself', whether their materialism is or is not pre-critical, etc. For all these questions are and always have been posed inside a certain *practice* of philosophy. The real question bears precisely on this traditional practice which Lenin brings back into question by proposing a *quite different* practice of philosophy.

This different practice contains something like a promise or outline of an *objective knowledge* of philosophy's mode of being. A knowledge of philosophy as a *Holzweg der Holzwege*. But the last thing philosophers and philosophy can bear, the intolerable, is perhaps precisely the idea of this knowledge. What philosophy cannot bear is the idea of a theory (i.e. of an objective knowledge) of philosophy capable of changing its traditional practice. Such a theory may be fatal for philosophy, since it lives by its denegation.

So academic philosophy cannot tolerate Lenin (or Marx for that matter) for two reasons, which are really one and the same. On the one hand, it cannot bear the idea that it might have something to learn from politics and from a politician. And on the other hand, it cannot bear the idea that philosophy might be the object of a theory, i.e. of an objective knowledge.

That *into the bargain*, it should be a politician like Lenin, an 'innocent' and an auto-didact in philosophy who had the audacity to suggest the idea that a theory of philosophy is essential to a really conscious and responsible *practice* of philosophy, is obviously too much. . . .

Here, too, philosophy, whether academic or otherwise, is not mistaken: it puts up such a stubborn resistance to this apparently accidental encounter in which a mere politician suggests to it the beginnings of a knowledge of what philosophy is, because this encounter *hits the mark*, the most sensitive point, the point of the intolerable, the point of the *repressed*, which traditionally philosophy has merely ruminated – precisely the point at which, in order to know itself in its theory, philosophy has to recognize that it is no more than a certain investment of politics, a certain continuation of politics, a certain rumination of politics.

Lenin happens to have been the first to say so. It also happens that he *could* say so only because he was a politician, and not just any politician, but a *proletarian leader*. That is why Lenin is intolerable to philosophical rumination, as intolerable – and I choose my words carefully – as Freud is to psychological rumination.

It is clear that between Lenin and established philosophy there are not just misunderstandings and incidental conflicts, not even just the philosophy professors' reactions of wounded sensibility when the son of a teacher, a petty lawyer who became a revolutionary leader, declares bluntly that most of them are petty-bourgeois intellectuals functioning in the bourgeois education system as so many ideologists inculcating the mass of student youth with the dogmas – however critical or post-critical – of the ideology of the ruling classes.[4] Between Lenin and established philosophy there is a peculiarly intolerable connexion: the connexion in which the reigning philosophy is touched to the quick of what it represses: politics.

4. See Appendix, p. 68 below.

3

But before we can really see how the relations between Lenin and philosophy reached this point, we must go back a little and, before discussing Lenin and philosophy in general, we have to establish Lenin's place in Marxist philosophy, and therefore to raise the question of the state of Marxist philosophy.

I cannot hope to outline the history of Marxist philosophy here. I am in no position to do so, and for an altogether determinant reason: I should have to know precisely what was this X whose history I proposed to write, and if I knew that, I would also have to be in a position to know whether this X has or has not a History, i.e. whether it has or has not the right to a History.

Rather than outlining, even very roughly, the 'history' of Marxist philosophy, I should like to demonstrate the existence of a symptomatic difficulty, in the light of a sequence of texts and works in History.

This difficulty has given rise to famous disputes which have lasted to the present day. The names most often given to these disputes signal its existence: what is the core of Marxist theory? a science or a philosophy? Is Marxism at heart a philosophy, the 'philosophy of praxis' – but then what of the scientific claims made by Marx? Is Marxism, on the contrary, at heart a science, historical materialism, the science of history – but then what of its philosophy, dialectical materialism? Or again, if we accept the classical distinction between historical materialism (science) and dialectical materialism (philosophy), how are we to think this distinction: in traditional terms or in new terms? Or again, what are the relations between materialism and the dialectic in dialectical materialism? Or again, what is the dialectic: a mere method? or philosophy as a whole?

This difficulty which has provided the fuel for so many disputes is a *symptomatic* one. This is intended to suggest that it is the evidence for a partly enigmatic reality, of which the classical questions that I have just recalled are a certain treatment, i.e. a certain interpretation. Speaking very schematically, the classical formulations interpret this difficulty solely in terms of *philosophical* questions, i.e. inside what I have called philosophical rumination – whereas it is undoubtedly necessary to think these difficulties and the philosophical questions which they cannot fail to provoke, in quite different terms: in terms of a *problem*, i.e. of objective (and therefore scientific) knowledge. Only on this condition, certainly, is it possible to understand the confusion that has led people to think in terms of prematurely philosophical questions the essential theoretical contribution of Marxism to philosophy, i.e. the insistence of a certain *problem* which may well produce philosophical effects, but only insofar as it is not itself in the last instance a philosophical *question*.

If I have deliberately used terms which presuppose certain distinctions (scientific problem, philosophical question), this is not so as to pass judgement on those who have been subject to this confusion, for we are all subject to it and we all have every reason to think that it was and still is inevitable – so much so that Marxist philosophy itself has been and still is caught in it, for necessary reasons.

For finally, a glance at the theatre of what is called Marxist philosophy since the *Theses on Feuerbach* is enough to show that it presents a rather curious spectacle. Granted that Marx's early works do not have to be taken into account (I know that this is to ask a concession which some people find difficult to accept, despite the force of the arguments I have put forward), and that we subscribe to Marx's statement that *The German Ideology* represented a decision to 'settle accounts with his erstwhile philosophical consciousness', and therefore a rupture and conversion in his thought, then when we examine what happens between the *Theses on Feuerbach* (the first indication of the 'break', *1845*) and Engels's *Anti-Dühring* (*1877*), the long interval of philosophical emptiness cannot fail to strike us.

The XIth Thesis on Feuerbach proclaimed: 'The philosophers have only interpreted the world in various ways; the point is to change it.' This simple sentence seemed to promise a new philosophy, one which was no longer an *interpretation*, but rather a *transformation* of the world. Moreover, that is how it was read more than half a century later, by Labriola, and then following him, by Gramsci, both of whom defined Marxism essentially as a new philosophy, a 'philosophy of praxis'. Yet we have to face the fact that this prophetic sentence produced no new philosophy immediately, at any rate, no new philosophical discourse, quite the contrary, it merely initiated a long philosophical silence. This silence was only broken publicly by what had all the appearances of an unforeseen accident: a precipitate intervention by Engels, forced to do ideological battle with Dühring, constrained to follow him onto his own 'territory' in order to deal with the political consequences of the 'philosophical' writings of a blind teacher of mathematics who was beginning to exercise a dangerous influence over German socialism.

Here we have a strange situation indeed: a Thesis which seems to announce a revolution in philosophy – then a thirty-year long philosophical silence, and finally a few improvised chapters of philosophical polemic published by Engels for political and ideological reasons as an introduction to a remarkable summary of Marx's scientific theories.

Must we conclude that we are the victims of a retrospective philosophical illusion when we read the XIth

Thesis on Feuerbach as the proclamation of a philosophical revolution? Yes and no. But *first* before saying no, I think it is necessary to say yes, seriously: *yes, we are essentially the victims of a philosophical illusion.* What was announced in the *Theses on Feuerbach* was, in the necessarily philosophical language of a declaration of rupture with all 'interpretative' philosophy, something quite different from a new philosophy: a new science, the science of history, whose first, still infinitely fragile foundations Marx was to lay in *The German Ideology.*

The philosophical emptiness which followed the proclamation of Thesis XI was thus the fullness of a science, the fullness of the intense, arduous and protracted labour which put an unprecedented science on to the stocks, a science to which Marx was to devote all his life, down to the last drafts for *Capital,* which he was never able to complete. It is this scientific fullness which represents the first and most profound reason why, even if Thesis XI did prophetically announce an event which was to make its mark on philosophy, it could not give rise to a philosophy, or rather *had* to proclaim the radical suppression of all existing philosophy in order to give priority to the work needed for the theoretical gestation of Marx's scientific discovery.

This radical suppression of philosophy is, as is well known, inscribed in so many words in *The German Ideology.* It is essential, says Marx in that work, to get rid of all philosophical fancies and turn to the study of positive reality, to tear aside the veil of philosophy and at last see reality for what it is.

The German Ideology bases this suppression of philosophy on a theory of philosophy as a hallucination and mystification, or to go further, as a *dream,* manufactured from what I shall call the day's residues of the real history of concrete men, day's residues endowed with a purely imaginary existence in which the order of things is inverted. Philosophy, like religion and ethics, is only ideology; it has no history, everything which seems to happen in it really happens outside it, in the only real history, the history of the material life of men. Science is then the real itself, known by the action which reveals it by destroying the ideologies that veil it: foremost among these ideologies is philosophy.

Let us halt at this dramatic juncture and explore its meaning. The theoretical revolution announced in Thesis XI is in reality the foundation of a new science. Employing a concept of Bachelard's, I believe we can think the theoretical event which inaugurates this new science as an 'epistemological break'.

Marx founds a new science, i.e. he elaborates a system of new scientific concepts where previously there prevailed only the manipulation of ideological notions. Marx founds the science of history where there were previously only philosophies of history. When I say that Marx organized a theoretical system of scientific concepts in the domain previously monopolized by philosophies of history, I am extending a metaphor which is no more than a metaphor: for it suggests that Marx replaced ideological theories with a scientific theory in a uniform space, that of History. In reality, this domain itself was reorganized. But with this crucial reservation, I propose to stick to the metaphor for the moment, and even to give it a still more precise form.

If in fact we consider the great scientific discoveries of human history, it seems that we might relate what we call *the sciences*, as a number of *regional* formations, to what I shall call the great theoretical *continents*. The distance that we have now obtained enables us, without anticipating a future which neither we nor Marx can 'stir in the pot', to pursue our improved metaphor and say that, before Marx, two continents *only* had been opened up to scientific knowledge by sustained epistemological breaks: the *continent of Mathematics* with the Greeks (by Thales or those designated by that mythical name) and the *continent of Physics* (by Galileo and his successors). A science like chemistry, founded by Lavoisier's epistemological break, is a regional science within the continent of physics: everyone now knows that it is inscribed in it. A science like biology, which came to the end of the first phase of its epistemological break, inaugurated by Darwin and Mendel, only a decade ago, by its integration with molecular chemistry, also becomes part of the continent of physics. Logic in its modern form becomes part of the continent of Mathematics, etc. On the other hand, it is probable that Freud's discovery has opened a new continent, one which we are only just beginning to explore.

If this metaphor stands up to the test of its extension, I can put forward the following proposition. Marx has opened up to scientific knowledge a new, third scientific continent, the continent of History, by an epistemological break whose first still uncertain strokes are inscribed in *The German Ideology*, after having been announced in the *Theses of Feuerbach*. Obviously this epistemological break is not an instantaneous event. It is even possible that one might, by recurrence and where some of its *details* are concerned, assign it a sort of premonition of a past. At any rate, this break becomes *visible* in its first signs, but these signs only inaugurate the beginning of an endless history. Like every break, this break is actually a sustained one within which complex reorganizations can be observed.

In fact, the operation of these reorganizations, which affect essential concepts and their theoretical components, can be observed empirically in the sequence of Marx's writings: in the *Manifesto* and *The Poverty of Philosophy* of 1847, in *A Contribution to the Critique of Political Economy* of 1859, in *Wages, Price and Profits* of 1865, in the first volume of *Capital* in 1867, etc. Other reorganizations and developments have followed, in the works of Lenin, especially in that unparalleled work of economic sociology, unfortunately ignored by sociologists, called *The Development of Capitalism in Russia*, in *Imperialism*, etc. Whether or no we accept the fact, we are still inscribed in the theoretical space marked and opened by this break today. Like the other breaks which opened up the other two continents that we know, this break inaugurates a history which will never come to an end.

That is why we should not read the XIth Thesis on Feuerbach as the announcement of a new philosophy, but as that necessary declaration of rupture with philosophy which clears the ground for the foundation of a new science. That is why from the radical suppression of all philosophy to the unforeseen 'accident' which induced the philosophical chapters in *Anti-Dühring*, there is a long philosophical silence during which only the new science speaks.

Of course, this new science is materialist, but so is every science, and that is why its general theory is called 'historical materialism'. Here materialism is quite simply the strict attitude of the scientist to the reality of his object which allows him to grasp what Engels called 'nature just as it exists without any foreign admixture'.

In the slightly odd phrase 'historical materialism' (we do not use the phrase 'chemical materialism' to designate chemistry), the word materialism registers both the initial rupture with the idealism of philosophies of history and the installation of scientificity with respect to history. Historical materialism thus means: science of history. If the birth of something like a Marxist philosophy is ever to be possible, it would seem that it must be from the very gestation of this science, a quite original sister, certainly, but in its very strangeness a sister of the existing sciences, after the long interval which always divides a philosophical reorganization from the scientific revolution which induced it.

Indeed, in order to go further into the reasons for this philosophical silence, I am driven to put forward a thesis concerning the relations between the sciences and philosophy without going further than to illustrate it with empirical data. Lenin began his book *State and Revolution* with this simple empirical comment: the State has not always existed; the existence of the State is only observable in class societies. In the same way, I shall say: philosophy has not always existed; the existence of philosophy is only observable in a world which contains what is called a science or a number of sciences. A science in the strict sense: a theoretical, i.e. ideal (*idéelle*) and demonstrative discipline, not an aggregate of empirical results.

Here in brief are my empirical illustrations of this thesis.

If philosophy is to be born, or reborn, one or more sciences must exist. Perhaps this is why philosophy in the strict sense only began with Plato, its birth induced by the existence of Greek Mathematics; was overhauled by Descartes, its modern revolution induced by Galilean physics; was recast by Kant under the influence of Newton's discovery; and was remodelled by Husserl under the impetus of the first axiomatics, etc.

I only suggest this theme, which needs to be tested, in order to point out, in the empirical mode still, that ultimately Hegel was not wrong to say that philosophy takes wing *at dusk*: when science, born at dawn, has already lived the time of a long day. Philosophy is thus always a long day behind the science which induces the birth of its first form and the rebirths of its revolutions, a long day which may last years, decades, a half-century or a century.

We should realize that the shock of a scientific break does

not make itself felt at once, that time is needed for it to reorganize philosophy.

We should also conclude, no doubt, that the work of philosophical gestation is closely linked with the work of scientific gestation, each being at work in the other. It is clear that the new philosophical categories are elaborated in the work of the new science. But it is also true that in certain cases (to be precise, Plato, Descartes) what is called philosophy also serves as a theoretical laboratory in which the new categories required by the concepts of the new science are brought into focus. For example, was it not in Cartesianism that a new category of causality was worked out for Galilean physics, which had run up against Aristotelian cause as an 'epistemological obstacle'? If we add to this the fact that the great philosophical events with which we are familiar (ancient philosophy descending from Plato, modern philosophy descending from Descartes) are clearly related to inducements from the opening of the two scientific continents, Greek Mathematics and Galilean Physics, we can pronounce (for this is all still emprical) certain inferences about what I think we can call Marxist philosophy. Three inferences:

First inference. If Marx really has opened up a new continent to scientific knowledge, his scientific discovery ought to induce some kind of important reorganization in philosophy. The XIth Thesis was perhaps ahead of its time, but it really did announce a major event in philosophy. It seems that this may be the case.

Second inference. Philosophy only exists by virtue of the distance it lags behind its scientific inducement. Marxist philosophy should therefore lag behind the Marxist science of history. This does indeed seem to be the case. The thirty-year desert between the *Theses on Feuerbach* and *Anti-Dühring* is evidence of this, as are certain long periods of deadlock later, periods in which we and many others are still marking time.

Third inference. There is a chance that we shall find more advanced theoretical elements for the elaboration of Marxist philosophy than we might have expected in the gestation of Marxist science, given the distance we now have on its lag. Lenin used to say that one should look in Marx's *Capital* for his dialectic – by which he meant Marxist philosophy itself. *Capital* must contain something from which to complete or forge the new philosophical categories: they are surely at work in *Capital*, in the 'practical state'. It seems that this may be the case. We must read *Capital* in order to find out.

The day is always long, but as luck would have it, it is already far advanced, look: dusk will soon fall. Marxist philosophy will take wing.

Taken as guide-lines, these inferences introduce, if I may say so, a kind of order into our concerns and hopes, and also into certain of our thoughts. We can now understand that the ultimate reason why Marx, trapped as he was in poverty, fanatical scientific work and the urgent demands of political leadership, never wrote the Dialectic (or Philosophy) he dreamed of, was not, *whatever he may have thought*, that he never 'found the time'. We can now understand that the ultimate reason why Engels, suddenly confronted with the necessity, as he writes, of 'having his say on philosophical questions', could not satisfy the professional philosophers, was not the improvised character of a merely ideological polemic. We can now understand that the ultimate reason for the philosophical limitations of *Materialism and Empirio-criticism* was not just a matter of the constraints of the ideological struggle.

We can now say it. The time that Marx could not find, Engels's philosophical extemporization, the laws of the ideological struggle in which Lenin was forced merely to turn his enemy's own weapons against him, each of these is a good enough excuse, but together they do not constitute a reason.

The ultimate reason is that the times were not ripe, that dusk had not yet fallen, and that neither Marx himself, nor Engels, nor Lenin could yet write the great work of philosophy which Marxism-Leninism lacks. If they did come well after the science on which it depends, in one way or another they all still came *too soon* for a philosophy, which is indispensable, but cannot be born without a necessary *lag*.

Given the concept of this necessary 'lag', everything should become clear, including the misunderstanding of those like the young Lukács and Gramsci, and so many others without their gifts, who were so impatient with the slowness of the birth of this philosophy that they proclaimed that it had already long been born, from the beginning, from the *Theses on Feuerbach*, i.e. well *before* the beginnings of Marxist science itself – and who, to prove this to themselves, simply stated that since every science is a 'superstructure', and every existing science is therefore basically positivist because it is bourgeois, Marxist 'science' could not but be *philosophical*, and Marxism a philosophy, a post-Hegelian philosophy or 'philosophy of praxis'.

Given the concept of this necessary 'lag', light can be cast on many other difficulties, too, even in the *political* history of Marxist organizations, their defeats and crises. If it is true, as the whole Marxist tradition claims, that the greatest event in the history of the class struggle – i.e. practically in human history – is the union of Marxist theory and the Workers' Movement, it is clear that the internal balance of that union may be threatened by those failures of theory known as *deviations*, however trivial they may be; we can understand the political scope of the unrelenting theoretical disputes unleased in the Socialist and then in the Communist Movement, over what Lenin calls mere 'shades of opinion', for, as he said in *What is to be done ?*: '*The fate of Russian Social-Democracy for very many years to come may depend on the strengthening of one or other "shade".*'

Therefore, Marxist theory being what it is, a science and a philosophy, and the philosophy having necessarily lagged behind the science, which has been hindered in its development by this, we may be tempted to think that these theoretical deviations were, at bottom, *inevitable*, not just because of the effects of the class struggle on and in theory, but also because of the dislocation (*décalage*) inside theory itself.

In fact, to turn to the past of the Marxist Workers' Movement, we can call by their real names the theoretical deviations which have led to the great historical defeats for the proletariat, that of the Second International, to mention only one. These deviations are called economism, evolutionism, voluntarism, humanism, empiricism, dogmatism, etc. Basically, these deviations are *philosophical* deviations, and were denounced as philosophical deviations by the great workers' leaders, starting with Engels and Lenin.

But this now brings us quite close to understanding why they overwhelmed even those who denounced them: were they not in some way inevitable, precisely as a function of the necessary *lag* of Marxist philosophy?

To go further, if this is the case, and even in the deep crisis today dividing the International Communist Movement, Marxist philosophers may well tremble before the task – unanticipated because so long anticipated – which history has assigned and entrusted to them. If it is true as so many signs indicate, that today the lag of Marxist philosophy can in part be overcome, doing so will not only cast light on the past, but also perhaps transform the future.

In this transformed future, justice will be done equitably to all those who had to live in the contradiction of political urgency and philosophical lag. Justice will be done to one of the greatest: to Lenin. Justice: his philosophical work will then be perfected. Perfected, i.e. completed and corrected. We surely owe this service and this homage to the man who was lucky enough to be born in time for politics, but unfortunate enough to be born too early for philosophy. After all, who chooses his own birth date?

4

Now that the 'history' of Marxist theory has shown us why Marxist philosophy lags behind the science of history, we can go directly to Lenin and into his work. But then our philosophical 'dream' will vanish: things do not have its simplicity.

Let me anticipate my conclusion. No, Lenin was not born too soon for philosophy. No one is ever born too soon for philosophy. If philosophy lags behind, if this lag is what makes it philosophy, how is it ever possible to lag behind a lag which has no history? If we absolutely must go on talking of a lag: it is we who are lagging behind Lenin. Our lag is simply another name for a mistake. For we are philosophically mistaken about the relations between Lenin and philosophy. The relations between Lenin and philosophy are certainly expressed *in* philosophy, inside the 'game' which constitutes philosophy as philosophy, but these relations are not philosophical, because this 'game' is not philosophical.

I want to try to expound the reasons for these conclusions

in a concise and systematic, and therefore necessarily schematic, form, taking as the object of my analysis Lenin's great 'philosophical' work: *Materialism and Empirio-criticism*. I shall divide this exposition into three moments:

1. *Lenin's great philosophical Theses.*
2. *Lenin and philosophical practice.*
3. *Lenin and partisanship in philosophy.*

In dealing with each of these points, I shall be concerned to show what was new in Lenin's contribution to Marxist theory.

I. LENIN'S GREAT PHILOSOPHICAL THESES

By Theses, I mean, like anyone else, the philosophical positions taken by Lenin, registered in philosophical pronouncements. For the moment I shall ignore the objection which has provided academic philosophy with a screen or pretext for its failure to read *Materialism and Empirio-criticism*: Lenin's categorial terminology, his historical references, and even his ignorances.

It is a fact itself worthy of a separate study that, even in the astonishing 'in lieu of an introduction' to *Materialism and Empirio-criticism* which takes us brusquely back to Berkeley and Diderot, Lenin in many respects situates himself in the *theoretical space of eighteenth-century empiricism*, i.e. in a philosophical problematic which is 'officially' pre-critical – if it is assumed that philosophy became 'officially' critical with Kant.

Once we have noted the existence of this reference system, once we know its structural logic, we can explain Lenin's theoretical formulations as so many effects of this logic, including the incredible contortions which he inflicts on the categorial terminology of empiricism in order to turn it against empiricism. For if he does think *in* the problematic of objective empiricism (Lenin even says 'objective sensualism') and if the fact of thinking in that problematic often affects not just the formulations of his thought, but even some of its movements, no one could deny that Lenin does *think*, i.e. thinks systematically and rigorously. It is this thought which matters to us, in that it pronounces certain Theses. Here they are, pronounced in their naked essentials. I shall distinguish three of them:

Thesis 1. Philosophy is not a science. Philosophy is distinct from the sciences. Philosophical categories are distinct from scientific concepts.

This is a crucial thesis. Let me indicate the decisive point in which its destiny is at stake: the category of *matter*, surely the touchstone for a materialist philosophy and for all the philosophical souls who hope for its salvation, i.e. its death. Now Lenin says in so many words that the distinction between the philosophical category of matter and the scientific concept of matter is vital for Marxist philosophy:

Matter is a philosophical category (Materialism and Empirio-criticism, p. 130).

The sole property of matter with whose recognition philosophical materialism is bound up is the property of being an objective reality (op. cit., pp. 260–61).

It follows that the philosophical *category* of matter, which is conjointly a Thesis of *existence* and a Thesis of *objectivity*, can never be confused with the contents of the scientific *concepts* of matter. The scientific concepts of matter define knowledges, relative to the historical state of the sciences, about the objects of those sciences. The content of the scientific concept of matter changes with the development, i.e. with the deepening of scientific knowledge. The meaning of the philosophical category of matter does not change, since it does not apply to any object of science, but affirms the *objectivity* of all scientific knowledge of an object. The category of *matter* cannot change. It is 'absolute'.

The consequences which Lenin draws from this distinction are crucial. Firstly, he re-establishes the truth about what was then called the 'crisis of physics': physics is not in crisis, but in growth. Matter has not 'disappeared'. The scientific concept of matter alone has *changed in content*, and it will always go on changing in the future, for the process of knowledge is infinite in its object itself.

The scientific pseudo-crisis of physics is only a *philosophical* crisis or fright in which ideologists, even though some of them are also scientists, are openly attacking materialism. When they proclaim the disappearance of matter, we should hear the silent discourse of their wish: *the disappearance of materialism!*

And Lenin denounces and knocks down all those ephemerally philosophical scientists who thought their time had come. What is left of these characters today? Who still remembers them? We must concede at least that this philosophical ignoramus Lenin had good judgement. And what professional philosopher was capable, as he was, of committing himself without hesitation or delay, so far and so surely, absolutely alone, against everyone, in an apparently lost cause? I should be grateful if anyone could give me one name – other than Husserl, at that time Lenin's objective ally against empiricism and historicism – but only a temporary ally and one who could not *meet* him, for Husserl, as a good 'philosopher', believed he was going 'somewhere'.

But Lenin's Thesis goes further than the immediate conjuncture. If it is absolutely essential to distinguish between the philosophical category of matter and every scientific concept, it follows that those materialists who apply philosophical categories to the objects of the sciences as if they were concepts of them are involved in a case of 'mistaken identity'. For example, anyone who wants to make *conceptual* use of *categorial* oppositions like matter/mind or matter/consciousness is only too likely to lapse into *tautology*, for the 'antithesis of matter and mind has absolute significance only within the bounds of a very limited field – in this case exclusively within the bounds of the fundamental epistemological problem of what is to be regarded as primary and what as secondary [i.e. in philosophy]. Beyond these bounds [i.e. in the sciences] the relative character of this antithesis is indubitable' (op. cit., p. 147).

I cannot go into other very wide-ranging consequences, e.g. into the fact that from Lenin's point of view the distinction between philosophy and the sciences necessarily opens up the field of a theory of the history of knowledges, or the fact that Lenin announces in his theory the historical *limits* of all truth (sc. all scientific knowledge) which he thinks as a theory of the distinction between *absolute truth and relative truth* (in this theory a single opposition of categories is used to think both the distinction between philosophy and the sciences, and the necessity for a theory of the history of the sciences).

I would just ask you to note what follows. The distinction between philosophy and the sciences, between philosophical categories and scientific concepts, constitutes at heart the adoption of a radical philosophical position *against all forms of empiricism and positivism*: against the empiricism and positivism even of certain materialists, against naturalism, against psychologism, against historicism (on this particular point see Lenin's polemical violence against Bogdanov's historicism).

It must be admitted that this is not so bad for a philosopher whom it is easy to dismiss as pre-critical and pre-

Kantian on the grounds of a few of his formulations, indeed, it is far rather astonishing, since it is clear that in 1908 this Bolshevik leader had never read a line of Kant and Hegel, but had stopped at Berkeley and Diderot. And yet, for some strange reason, he displays a 'critical' feeling for his positivist opponents and a remarkable strategic discernment within the religious concert of the 'hyper-critical' philosophy of his day.

The most amazing thing of all is the fact that Lenin manages the *tour de force* of taking up these *anti-empiricist positions precisely in the field of an empiricist reference problematic*. It certainly is a paradoxical exploit to manage to be anti-empiricist while thinking and expressing oneself in the basic categories of empiricism, and must surely pose a slight 'problem' for any philosopher of good faith who is prepared to examine it.

Does this by any chance mean that the field of the philosophical problematic, its categorial formulations and its philosophical pronouncements are relatively indifferent to the philosophical positions adopted? Does it mean that at heart nothing essentially happens in what seems to constitute philosophy? Strange.

Thesis 2. If philosophy is distinct from the sciences, there is a privileged link between philosophy and the sciences. This link is represented by the materialist thesis of objectivity.

Here, two points are essential.

The first concerns the nature of scientific knowledge. The suggestions contained in *Materialism and Empirio-criticism* are taken up, developed and deepened in the *Philosophical Notebooks*: they give their full meaning to the anti-empiricism and anti-positivism which Lenin shows within his conception of *scientific practice*. In this respect, Lenin must also be regarded as a witness who speaks of scientific practice as a genuine practitioner. A reading of the texts he devoted to Marx's *Capital* between 1898 and 1905, and his analysis of *The Development of Capitalism in Russia* is enough to show that his scientific practice as a Marxist theoretician of history, political economy and sociology was constantly accompanied by acute epistemological reflections which his philosophical texts simply take up in a generalized form.

What Lenin reveals, and here again, using categories which may be contaminated by his empiricist references (e.g. the category of reflection), is the anti-empiricism of scientific practice, the decisive role of scientific abstraction, or rather, the role of conceptual systematicity, and in a more general way, the role of theory as such.

Politically, Lenin is famous for his critique of 'spontaneism', which, it should be noted, is not directed against the spontaneity, resourcefulness, inventiveness and genius of the masses of the people but against a political ideology which, screened by an exaltation of the spontaneity of the masses, exploits it in order to divert it into an incorrect politics. But it is not generally realized that Lenin adopts exactly the same position in his conceptions of scientific practice. Lenin wrote: *'without revolutionary theory there can be no revolutionary movement.'* He could equally have written: *without scientific theory there can be no production of scientific knowledges.* His defence of the requirements of theory in scientific practice precisely coincides with his defence of the requirements of theory in political practice. His anti-spontaneism then takes the theoretical form of anti-empiricism, anti-positivism and anti-pragmatism.

But just as his political anti-spontaneism presupposes the deepest respect for the spontaneity of the masses, his theoretical anti-spontaneism presupposes the greatest respect for *practice* in the process of knowledge. Neither in his conception of science, nor in his conception of politics does Lenin for one moment fall into *theoreticism*.

This first point enables us to understand the *second*. Materialist philosophy is, in Lenin's eyes, profoundly linked to scientific practice. This thesis must, I believe, be understood in two senses.

First in an extremely classical sense which illustrates what we have been able to observe empirically in the history of the relations which link all philosophy to the sciences. For Lenin, what happens in the sciences is a crucial concern of philosophy. The great scientific revolutions induce important reorganizations in philosophy. This is Engels's famous thesis: materialism changes in form with each great scientific discovery. Engels was fascinated by the philosophical consequences of discoveries in the natural sciences (the cell, evolution, Carnot's principle, etc.), but Lenin defends the same thesis in a better way by showing that the decisive discovery which has induced an obligatory reorganization of materialist philosophy does not come so much from the sciences of nature as from the *science of history*, from historical materialism.

In a second sense, Lenin invokes an important argument. Here he no longer talks of philosophy in general, but of materialist philosophy. The latter is particularly concerned with what happens in scientific practice, but in a manner peculiar to itself, because it *represents*, in its materialist thesis, the *'spontaneous'* convictions of scientists about the existence of the objects of their sciences, and the objectivity of their knowledge.

In *Materialism and Empirio-criticism*, Lenin constantly repeats the statement that most specialists in the sciences of nature are 'spontaneously' materialistic, at least in *one of the tendencies* of their spontaneous philosophy. While fighting the ideologies of the spontaneism of scientific practice (empiricism, pragmatism), Lenin recognizes in the experience of scientific practice a spontaneous materialist tendency of the highest importance for Marxist philosophy. He thus interrelates the materialist theses required to think the specificity of scientific *knowledge* with the spontaneous materialist tendency of the *practitioners* of the sciences: as expressing both practically and theoretically one and the same materialist thesis of existence and objectivity.

Let me anticipate and say that the Leninist insistence on affirming the privileged link between the sciences and Marxist materialist philosophy is evidence that here we are dealing with a decisive nodal point, which, if I may, I shall call *Nodal Point No. 1*.

But precisely in this mention of the spontaneous philosophy of the scientist something important is emerging which will bring us to another decisive nodal point of a quite different kind.

Thesis 3. Here, too, Lenin is taking up a classical thesis expounded by Engels in *Ludwig Feuerbach and the End of Classical German Philosophy*, but he gives it an unprecedented scope. This thesis concerns the history of philosophy conceived as the history of an age-old struggle between two tendencies: idealism and materialism.

It must be admitted that in its bluntness, this thesis runs directly counter to the convictions of the great majority of professional philosophers. If they are prepared to read Lenin, and they will all have to some day, they will all admit that his philosophical theses are not so summary as reputation makes them. But I am afraid that they will stubbornly resist this last thesis, for it threatens to wound them in their most profound convictions. It appears far too crude, fit only for public, i.e. ideological and political, disputes. To say that the whole history of philosophy can be reduced in the last instance to a struggle between materialism and idealism seems to cheapen all the wealth of the history of philosophy.

In fact, this thesis amounts to the claim that essentially *philosophy has no real history*. What is a history which is no more than the repetition of the clash between two fundamental tendencies? The forms and arguments of the fight may vary, but if the whole history of philosophy is merely the history of these forms, they only have to be reduced to the immutable tendencies that they represent for the transformation of these forms to become a kind of *game for nothing*. Ultimately, philosophy has no history, philosophy is that strange theoretical site where nothing really happens, nothing but this *repetition* of nothing. To say that nothing happens in philosophy is to say that philosophy *leads nowhere because it is going nowhere*: the paths it opens really are, as Dietzgen said, long before Heidegger, '*Holzwege*', paths that lead nowhere.

Besides, that is what Lenin suggests *in practice*, when, right at the beginning of *Materialism and Empirio-criticism*, he explains that Mach merely *repeats* Berkeley, and himself counterposes to this his own *repetition* of Diderot. Worse still, it is clear that Berkeley and Diderot *repeat* each other, since they are in agreement about the matter/mind opposition, merely arranging its terms in a different way. The nothing of their philosophy is only the nothing of this inversion of the terms in an immutable categorial opposition (Matter/Mind) which represents in philosophical theory the play of the two antagonistic tendencies in confrontation in this opposition. The history of philosophy is thus nothing but the nothing of this repeated inversion. In addition, this thesis would restore a meaning to the famous phrases about Marx's inversion of Hegel, the Hegel whom Engels himself described as no more than a previous inversion.

On this point it is essential to recognize that Lenin's

insistence has absolutely no limits. In *Materialism and Empirio-criticism*, at least (for his tone changes on this point in the *Philosophical Notebooks*), he jettisons all the theoretical nuances, distinctions, ingenuities and subtleties with which philosophy tries to think its 'object': they are nothing but sophistries, hair-splitting, professorial quibbles, accommodations and compromises whose only aim is to mask what is really at stake in the dispute to which all philosophy is committed: the basic struggle between the tendencies of materialism and idealism. There is no third way, no half-measure, no bastard position, any more than there is in politics. Basically, there are only idealists and materialists. All those who do not openly declare themselves one or the other are 'shame-faced' materialists or idealists (Kant, Hume).

But we must therefore go even further and say that if the whole history of philosophy is nothing but the re-examination of arguments in which one and the same struggle is carried to its conclusion, then philosophy is nothing but a tendency struggle, the *Kampfplatz* that Kant discussed, which however, throws us back onto the subjectivity pure and simple of ideological struggles. It is to say that *philosophy strictly speaking has no object*, in the sense that a science has an object.

Lenin goes as far as this, which proves that Lenin was a *thinker*. He declares that it is impossible to prove the ultimate principles of materialism just as it is impossible to prove (or refute, to Diderot's annoyance) the principles of idealism. It is impossible to prove them because they cannot be the object of a knowledge, meaning by that a knowledge comparable with that of science which does prove the properties of its objects.

So philosophy has no object. But now everything fits. If nothing happens in philosophy it is precisely because it has no object. If something actually does happen in the sciences, it is because they do have an object, knowledge of which they can increase, *which gives them a history*. As philosophy has no object, nothing can happen in it. The nothing of its history simply repeats the nothing of its object.

Here we are beginning to get close to *Nodal Point No. 2*, which concerns these famous *tendencies*. Philosophy merely re-examines and ruminates over arguments which represent the basic conflict of these tendencies in the form of categories. It is their conflict, unnameable *in* philosophy, which sustains the eternal null inversion for which philosophy is the garrulous theatre, the inversion of the fundamental categorial opposition between matter and mind. How then is the tendency revealed? In the hierarchic order it installs between the terms of the opposition: an order of domination. Listen to Lenin:

Bogdanov, pretending to argue only against Beltov and cravenly ignoring Engels, is indignant at such *definitions*, which, don't you see, 'prove to be simple *repetitions*' of the 'formula' (of Engels, our 'Marxist' forgets to add) that for one trend in philosophy matter is primary and spirit secondary, while for the other trend the reverse is the case. All the Russian Machists exultantly echo Bogdanov's 'refutation'! But the slightest reflection could have shown these people that *it is impossible, in the very nature of the case, to give any definition of these two ultimate concepts of epistemology, except an indication which of them is taken as primary.* What is meant by giving a 'definition'? It means essentially to bring a given concept within a more comprehensive concept. . . . The question then is, are there more comprehensive concepts with which the theory of knowledge could operate than those of being and thinking, matter and sensation, physical and mental? No. These are the ultimate, most comprehensive concepts, which epistemology has in point of fact so far not surpassed (apart from changes in *nomenclature*, which are always possible). One must be a charlatan or an utter blockhead *to demand a 'definition' of these two 'series' of concepts of ultimate comprehensiveness which would not be a 'mere repetition': one or the other must be taken as primary* (*Materialism and Empirio-criticism*, p. 146).

The inversion which is formally the nothing which happens in philosophy, in its explicit discourse, is not null, or rather, it is an effect of annulment, the annulment of a previous hierarchy replaced by the opposite hierarchy. What is at stake in philosophy in the ultimate categories which govern all philosophical systems, is therefore the sense of this hierarchy, the sense of this location of one category in the dominant position, it is something in philosophy which irresistibly recalls a seizure of power or an *installation in power*. Philosophically, we should say: an installation in power is without an *object*. An installation in power, is this still a purely theoretical category? A seizure of power (or an installation in power) is political, it does not have an object, it has a stake, precisely the power, and an aim: the effects of that power.

Here we should stop for a moment to see what is new in Lenin's contribution with respect to Engels's. His contribution is enormous if we are really prepared to weigh up the effects of something which has to often been taken for a mere shade of opinion.

Ultimately, although Engels has strokes of astonishing genius when he is working on Marx, his *thought* is not comparable with Lenin's. Often he only manages to juxtapose theses – rather than managing to *think* them in the unity of their relations.

Worse still: he never really rid himself of a certain positivist theme from *The German Ideology*. For although he recommends its systematic study, for him philosophy has to disappear: it is merely the craftsman's laboratory in which the philosophical categories necessary to science were forged in the past. These times have gone. Philosophy has done its work. Now it must give way to science. Since the sciences are scientifically capable of presenting *the organic unitary system of their relations*, there is no longer any need either for a *Naturphilosophie* or for a *Geschichts-philosophie*.

What is left for philosophy? An object: the dialectic, the most general laws of nature (but the sciences provide them) and of thought. There thus remains the laws of thought which can be disengaged from the history of the sciences. Philosophy is thus not really separate from the sciences, hence the positivism that insinuates itself into certain of Engels's formulations, when he says that to be a materialist is to admit nature as it is 'without any foreign admixture', despite the fact that he knows that the sciences are a process of knowledge. That is why philosophy does have an object for all that: but paradoxically, it is then *pure thought*, which would not displease idealism. For example, what else is Lévi-Strauss up to today, on his own admission, and by appeal to Engels's authority? He, too, is studying the laws, let us say the structures *of thought*. Ricœur has pointed out to him, correctly, that he is Kant minus the transcendental subject. Lévi-Strauss has not denied it. Indeed, if the object of philosophy is pure thought, it is possible to appeal to Engels and find oneself a Kantian, minus the trans-cendental subject.

The same difficulty can be expressed in another way. The dialectic, the object of philosophy, is called a *logic*. Can philosophy really have the object of Logic for its object? It seems that Logic is now moving further and further away from philosophy: it is a science.

Of course, *at the same time*, Engels also defends the thesis of the two tendencies, but materialism and dialectics on the one hand, tendency struggle and philosophical advance exclusively determined by scientific advance on the other hand are two things very hard to think together, i.e. to *think*. Engels tries, but even if we are prepared not to take him literally (the least that can be asked where a non-specialist is concerned) it is only too clear that he is *missing* something *essential*.

Which is to say that he is *missing* something essential to his thought if he is to be able to think. Thanks to Lenin we can see that this is a matter of an *omission*. For Engels's thought is missing precisely what Lenin adds to it.

Lenin contributes a profoundly consistent thought, in which are located a number of radical theses that undoubtedly circumscribe emptinesses, but precisely *pertinent* emptinesses. At the centre of his thought is the thesis that philosophy *has no object*, i.e. philosophy is not to be explained merely *by the relationship it maintains with the sciences*.

We are getting close to *Nodal Point No. 2*. But we have not got there yet.

2. LENIN AND PHILOSOPHICAL PRACTICE

In order to reach this *Nodal Point No. 2*, I shall enter a new domain, that of philosophical practice. It would be interesting to study Lenin's philosophical practice in his various works. But that would presuppose that we already knew what philosophical practice is as such.

Now it so happens that on a few rare occasions, Lenin was forced by the exigencies of philosophical polemic to produce a kind of *definition of his philosophical practice*. Here are the two clearest passages:

> You will say that this distinction between relative and absolute truth is indefinite. And I shall reply: it is sufficiently 'indefinite' *to prevent science from becoming a dogma in the bad sense of the term*, from becoming something dead, frozen, ossified; but at the same time it is sufficiently 'definite' to enable us to *draw a dividing-line in the most emphatic and irrevocable manner* between ourselves and fideism and agnosticism, between ourselves and philosophical idealism and the

sophistry of the followers of Hume and Kant' (*Materialism and Empirio-criticism*, p. 136).

Of course, we must not forget that the criterion of practice can never, in the nature of things, either confirm or refute any human idea completely. This criterion too is sufficiently 'indefinite' not to allow human knowledge to become 'absolute', but at the same time it is sufficiently definite to wage a ruthless fight on all varieties of idealism and agnosticism (op. cit., pp. 142–3).

Other passages confirm Lenin's position. These are clearly not rash or isolated formulations, but the expressions of a profound thought.

Lenin thus defines the ultimate essence of philosophical practice as an *intervention* in the theoretical domain. This intervention takes a double form: it is theoretical in its formulation of definite categories; and practical in the function of these categories. This function consists of 'drawing a dividing-line' inside the theoretical domain between ideas declared to be true and ideas declared to be false, between the scientific and the ideological. The effects of this line are of two kinds: positive in that they assist a certain practice – scientific practice – and negative in that they defend this practice against the dangers of certain ideological notions: here those of idealism and dogmatism. Such, at least, are the effects produced by *Lenin's* philosophical intervention.

In this drawing of a dividing-line we can see the two basic tendencies we have discussed confronting one another. It is materialist philosophy that draws this dividing-line, in order to protect scientific practice against the assaults of idealist philosophy, the scientific against the assaults of the ideological. We can generalize this definition by saying: all philosophy consists of drawing a major dividing-line by means of which it repels the ideological notions of the philosophies that represent the opposing tendency; the stake in this act of drawing, i.e. in philosophical practice, is scientific practice, scientificity. Here we rediscover my *Nodal Point No. 1*: the privileged relation of philosophy to the sciences.

We also rediscover the paradoxical game of the inversion of terms in which the history of philosophy is annulled in the nothing it produces. This nothing is not null: since its stake is the fate of the scientific practices, of the scientific, and of its partner, the ideological. Either the scientific practices are exploited or they are assisted by the philosophical intervention.

We can thus understand why philosophy can have a history, and yet nothing occurs in that history. For the intervention of each philosophy, which displaces or modifies existing philosophical categories and thus produces those changes in philosophical discourse in which the history of philosophy proffers its existence, is precisely the philosophical nothing whose insistence we have established, since a dividing-line actually is nothing, it is not even a line or a drawing, but the simple fact of being divided, i.e. *the emptiness of a distance taken*.

This distance leaves its *trace* in the distinctions of the philosophical discourse, in its modified categories and apparatus; but all these modifications are nothing in themselves since they only act outside their own presence, in the distance or non-distance which separates the antagonistic tendencies from the scientific practices, the stake in their struggle.

All that can be truly philosophical in this operation of a null drawing is its displacement, but that is relative to the history of the scientific practices and of the sciences. For there is a history of the sciences, and the lines of the philosophical front are displaced according to the transformations of the scientific conjuncture (i.e. according to the state of the sciences and their problems), and according to the state of the philosophical apparatuses that these transformations induce. The terms that designate the scientific and the ideological thus have to be *re-thought* again and again.

Hence there is a history *in* philosophy rather than a history *of* philosophy: a history of the displacement of the indefinite repetition of a null trace whose effects are real. This history can be read profitably in all the great philosophers, even the idealist ones – and in the one who sums up the whole history of philosophy, Hegel. That is why Lenin read Hegel, with astonishment – but this reading of Hegel is also a part of Lenin's *philosophical practice*. To read Hegel as a materialist is to draw dividing-lines within him.

No doubt I have gone beyond Lenin's literal meaning, but I do not think that I have been unfaithful to him. At any rate, I say simply that Lenin offers us something with which we can begin to think the specific form of *philosophical practice* in its essence, and give a meaning retrospectively to a number of formulations contained in the great texts of classical philosophy. For, in his own way, Plato had already discussed the struggle between the Friends of the Forms and the Friends of the Earth, declaring that the true philosopher must know how to demarcate, incise and draw dividing-lines.

However, one fundamental question remains: what of the two great tendencies which confront one another in the history of philosophy? Lenin gives this question a wild answer (*une réponse sauvage*), but an answer.

3. PARTISANSHIP IN PHILOSOPHY

The answer is contained in the thesis – famous, and it must be said, shocking to many people – of partisanship in philosophy.

This word sounds like a *directly* political slogan in which partisan means a political party, the Communist Party.

And yet, any half-way close reading of Lenin, not only of *Materialism and Empirio-criticism*, but also and above all of his analyses in the theory of history and of the economy, will show that it is a concept and not just a slogan.

Lenin is simply observing that all philosophy is partisan, as a function of its basic tendency, against the opposing basic tendency, via the philosophies which represent it. But at the same time, he is observing that the vast majority of philosophers put a great price on being able to declare publicly and prove that *they are not partisan because they do not have to be partisan.*

Thus Kant: the '*Kampfplatz*' he discusses is all right for other, pre-critical philosophers, but not for critical philosophy. His own philosophy is outside the '*Kampfplatz*', somewhere else, whence it assigns itself precisely the function of arbitrating the conflicts of metaphysics in the name of the interests of Reason. Ever since philosophy began, from Plato's $\Theta \epsilon \omega \rho \epsilon \hat{\iota} \nu$ to Husserl's philosopher as 'civil servant of humanity', and even to Heidegger in some of his writings, the history of philosophy has also been dominated by this repetition, which is the repetition of a contradiction: *the theoretical denegation of its own practice, and enormous theoretical efforts to register this degenation in consistent discourses.*

Lenin's response to this surprising fact, which seems to be constitutive of the vast majority of philosophies, is simply to say a *few words* to us about the insistence of these mysterious tendencies in confrontation in the history of philosophy. In Lenin's view, these tendencies are finally related to class positions and therefore to class conflicts. I say *related to* (*en rapport*), for Lenin says no more than that, and besides, he never says that philosophy can be reduced to the class struggle pure and simple, or even to what the Marxist tradition calls the ideological class struggle. Not to go beyond Lenin's declarations, we can say that, in his view, philosophy *represents* the class struggle, i.e. politics. It *represents* it, which presupposes *an instance with* (*auprès de*) *which* politics is thus represented: this instance is the sciences.

Nodal Point No. 1: the relation between philosophy and the sciences. *Nodal Point No. 2*: the relationship between philosophy and politics. Everything revolves around this double relation.

We can now advance the following proposition: philosophy is a certain continuation of politics, in a certain domain, *vis-à-vis* a certain reality. Philosophy represents politics in the domain of theory, or to be more precise: *with the sciences* – and, *vice versa*, philosophy represents scientificity in politics, with the classes engaged in the class struggle. How this representation is governed, by what mechanisms this representation is assured, by what mechanisms it can be falsified or faked and *is falsified as a general rule*, Lenin does not tell us. He is clearly profoundly convinced that in the last resort no philosophy can run ahead of this condition, evade the determinism of this double representation. In other words, he is convinced that philosophy exists somewhere as a third instance between the two major instances which constitute it as itself an instance: the class struggle and the sciences.

One more word is enough: if *Nodal Point No. 1*, the instance of the Sciences, is to be found in Engels, *Nodal*

Point No. 2, the instance of Politics, is not, despite his mention of tendency struggles in philosophy. In other words, Lenin is not just a commentator of Engels; he has contributed something new and decisive in what is called the domain of Marxist philosophy: what was *missing* from Engels.

One more word and we are through. For the knowledge of this double representation of philosophy is only the hesitant beginning of a *theory of philosophy*, but it really is such a beginning. No one will dispute the fact that this theory is an embryonic one, that it has hardly even been outlined in what we thought was a mere polemic. At least these suggestions of Lenin's, if accepted, have the unexpected result that they *displace the question into a problem*, and remove what is called Marxist philosophy from the rumination of a philosophical practice which has always and absolutely predominately been that of the *denegation* of its real practice.

That is how Lenin responded to the prophecy in the XIth Thesis, and he was the first to do so, for no one had done it before him, not even Engels. He himself responded in the 'style' of his philosophical practice. A wild practice (*une pratique sauvage*) in the sense in which Freud spoke of a wild analysis, one which does not provide the theoretical credentials for its operations and which raises screams from the philosophy of the 'interpretation' of the world, which might be called the philosophy of *denegation*. A wild practice, if you will, but what did not begin by being wild?

The fact is that this practice is a *new* philosophical practice: *new* in that it is no longer that rumination which is no more than the practice of denegation, where philosophy, constantly intervening 'politically' in the disputes in which the real destiny of the sciences is at stake, between the scientific that they install and the ideology that threatens them, and constantly intervening 'scientifically' in the struggle in which the fate of the classes is at stake, between the scientific that assists them and the ideological that threatens them – nonetheless stubbornly denies in philosophical 'theory' that it is intervening in these ways: *new* in that it is a practice which has renounced denegation, and, knowing what it does, *acts according to what it is*.

If this is indeed the case, we may surely suspect that it is no accident that this unprecedented effect was induced by Marx's *scientific* discovery, and thought by a *proletarian political* leader. For if philosophy's birth was induced by the first science in human history, this happened in Greece, in a class society, and knowing just how far class exploitation's effects may stretch, we should not be astonished that these effects, too, took a form which is classical in class societies, in which the ruling classes *denegate* the fact that they rule, the form of a philosophical denegation of philosophy's domination by politics. We should not be astonished that only the scientific knowledge of the mechanisms of class rule and all their effects, which Marx produced and Lenin applied, induced the extraordinary displacement in philosophy that shatters the phantasms of the denegation in which philosophy tells itself, so that men will believe it and so as to believe it itself, that it is above politics, just as it is above classes.

Only with Lenin, then, could the prophetic sentence in the XIth Thesis on Feuerbach at last acquire body and meaning. (Until now) 'the philosophers have interpreted the world in various ways; the point is to change it'. Does this sentence promise a new *philosophy*? I do not think so. Philosophy will not be suppressed: philosophy will remain philosophy. But knowing what its practice is and knowing what it is, or beginning to know it, it can be slowly transformed by this knowledge. Less than ever can we say that

Marxism is a new philosophy: a philosophy of praxis. At the heart of Marxist theory, there is a science: a quite unique science, but a science. What is new in Marxism's contribution to philosophy is a new *practice of philosophy*. *Marxism is not a (new) philosophy of praxis, but a (new) practice of philosophy.*

This new practice of philosophy can transform philosophy. And in addition it can to some extent *assist* in the transformation of the world. Assist only, for it is not theoreticians, scientists or philosophers, nor is it 'men', who make history – but the 'masses', i.e. the classes allied in a single class struggle.

February 1968

APPENDIX

To avoid any misunderstanding of the meaning of this condemnation of philosophy teachers and of the philosophy that they teach, attention should be paid to the date of the text and to certain of its expressions. Echoing Dietzgen, Lenin condemns philosophy teachers *as a mass*, not all philosophy teachers without exception. He condemns their philosophy, but he does not condemn philosophy. He even recommends the *study* of their philosophy, so as to be able to define and pursue a different practice than theirs in philosophy. A triple observation, therefore, in which in the end the date and circumstances change nothing of substance.

1. Philosophy teachers are teachers, i.e. intellectuals employed in a given education system and subject to that system, performing, as a mass, the social function of inculcating the 'values of the ruling ideology'. The fact

that there may be a certain amount of 'play' in schools and other institutions, which enables individual teachers to turn their teaching and reflection against these established 'values' does not change the *mass* effect of the philosophical teaching function. Philosophers are intellectuals and therefore petty bourgeois, subject as a mass to bourgeois and petty-bourgeois ideology.

2. That is why the ruling philosophy, whose representatives or supports the mass of philosophy teachers are, even in their 'critical' freedom, is subject to the ruling ideology, defined by Marx from *The German Ideology* on as the ideology of the ruling class. This ideology is dominated by idealism.

3. This situation, shared by those petty-bourgeois intellectuals, the philosophy teachers, and by the philosophy they teach or reproduce in their own individual form, does not mean that it is impossible for certain intellectuals to escape the constraints that dominate the mass of intellectuals, and, if philosophers, to adhere to a materialist philosophy and a revolutionary theory. The *Communist Manifesto* itself evoked the possibility. Lenin returns to it, adding that the collaboration of these intellectuals is indispensable to the Workers' Movement. On 7 February 1908, he wrote to Gorky: 'The significance of the intellectuals in our Party is declining; news comes from all sides that the intelligentsia is fleeing the Party. And a good riddance to these scoundrels. The Party is purging itself from petty-bourgeois dross. The workers are having a bigger say in things. The role of the worker-professionals is increasing. All this is wonderful.' Gorky, whose cooperation Lenin was asking for, protested, so Lenin replied on 13 February 1908: 'I think that some of the questions you raise about our differences of opinion are a sheer misunderstanding. Never, of course, have I thought of "chasing away the

intelligentsia" as the silly syndicalists do, or of denying its necessity for the Workers' Movement. There can be no divergence between us on any of these questions.' On the other hand, in the same letter, the philosophical divergences persist: 'It is in regard to materialism as a world outlook that I think I disagree with you in substance.' This is hardly surprising, for Gorky was pleading the cause of empirio-criticism and neo-Kantianism.

Preface to *Capital* Volume One

Now, for the first time in the history of French publishing, *Capital* Volume One is available to a mass audience.

What is *Capital*?

It is Marx's greatest work, the one to which he devoted his whole life after 1850, and to which he sacrificed the better part of his personal and family existence in bitter tribulation.

This work is the one by which Marx has to be *judged*. By it alone, and not by his still idealist 'Early Works' (1841–1844); not by still very ambiguous works like *The German Ideology*,[1] or even the *Grundrisse*, drafts which have been translated into French under the erroneous title '*Fondements* de le Critique de l'Économie Politique' (Foundations of the critique of political economy);[2] not even by the famous *Preface* to *A Contribution to the Critique of Political Economy*,[3] where Marx defines the 'dialectic' of the

1. 1845. A work which remained unpublished in Marx's lifetime. English-language translation published by International Publishers, New York, 1947.
2. The 'Grundrisse', manuscripts written by Marx in 1857–59. French translation published by Éditions Anthropos, Paris. [No full English translation as yet – Translator's Note.]
3. *Preface* to *A Contribution to the Critique of Political Economy* (1859), published by International Publishers, New York, 1971.

'correspondence and non-correspondence' between the Productive Forces and the Relations of Production in very ambiguous (because Hegelian) terms.

Capital, a mighty work, contains what is simply one of the three great scientific discoveries of the whole of human history: the discovery of the system of concepts (and therefore of the *scientific theory*) which opens up to scientific knowledge what can be called the 'Continent of History'. Before Marx, two 'continents' of comparable importance had been 'opened up' to scientific knowledge: the Continent of Mathematics, by the Greeks in the fifth century B.C., and the Continent of Physics, by Galileo.

We are still very far from having assessed the extent of this decisive discovery and drawn all the theoretical conclusions from it. In particular, the specialists who work in the domains of the 'Human Sciences' and of the Social Sciences (a smaller domain), i.e. economists, historians, sociologists, social psychologists, psychologists, historians of art and literature, of religious and other ideologies – and even linguists and psycho-analysts, all these specialists ought to know that they cannot produce truly scientific knowledges in their specializations unless they recognize the indispensability of the theory Marx founded. For it is, in principle, the theory which 'opens up' to scientific knowledge the 'continent' in which they work, in which they have so far only produced a few preliminary knowledges (linguistics, psycho-analysis) or a few elements or rudiments of knowledge (the occasional chapter of history, sociology and economics) or illusions pure and simple, illegitimately called knowledges.

Only the militants of the proletarian class struggle have drawn the conclusions from *Capital*: they have recognized its account of the mechanisms of capitalist exploitation, and grouped themselves in the organizations of the economic class struggle (the trade unions) and of the political class struggle (the Socialist, then Communist Parties), which apply a mass 'line' of struggle for the seizure of State Power, a 'line' based on 'the concrete analysis of the concrete situation' (Lenin) in which they have to fight (this 'analysis' being achieved by a correct application of Marx's scientific concepts to the 'concrete situation').

It is paradoxical that highly 'cultivated' intellectual specialists have not understood a book which contains the Theory which they need in their 'disciplines' and that, inversely, the militants of the Workers' Movement have understood this same Book, despite its great difficulties. The paradox is easy to explain, and the explanation of it is given word for word by Marx in *Capital* and by Lenin in his works.[4]

If the workers have 'understood' *Capital* so easily it is because it speaks in scientific terms of the everyday reality with which they are concerned: the exploitation which they suffer because of the capitalist system. That is why *Capital* so rapidly became the 'Bible' of the International Workers' Movement, as Engels said in 1886. Inversely, the specialists in history, political economy, sociology, psychology, etc., have had and still have such trouble 'understanding' *Capital* because they are subject to the ruling ideology (the ideology of the ruling class) which intervenes directly in their 'scientific' practice, falsifying their objects, their theories and their methods. With a few exceptions, they do not suspect, they cannot suspect the extraordinary power and variety of the ideological grip to which they are subject in their 'practice' itself. With a few exceptions, they are not in a position to criticize for themselves the illusions in

4. See for example the beginning of Lenin's *State and Revolution*, in *Selected Works*, International Publishers, New York, 1967.

which they live and to whose maintenance they contribute, because they are literally blinded by them. With a few exceptions, they are not in a position to carry out the ideological and theoretical *revolution* which is necessary if they are to recognize in Marx's theory the very theory their practice needs in order to become at last scientific.

When we speak of the difficulty of *Capital*, it is therefore essential to apply a distinction of the greatest importance. Reading *Capital* in fact presents two types of difficulty which have nothing to do with each other.

Difficulty No. 1, absolutely and massively determinant, is an ideological difficulty, and therefore in the last resort a *political* difficulty.

Two sorts of readers confront *Capital*: those who have direct experience of capitalist exploitation (above all the proletarians or wage-labourers in direct production, but also, with nuances according to their place in the production system, the non-proletarian wage-labourers); and those who have no direct experience of capitalist exploitation, but who are, on the contrary, ruled in their practices and consciousness by the ideology of the ruling class, bourgeois ideology. The first have no ideologico-political difficulty in understanding *Capital* since it is a straightforward discussion of their concrete lives. The second have great difficulty in understanding *Capital* (even if they are very 'scholarly', I would go so far as to say, especially if they are very 'scholarly'), because there is a *political incompatibility* between the theoretical content of *Capital* and the ideas they carry in their heads, ideas which they 'rediscover' in their practices (because they put them there in the first place). That is why Difficulty No. 1 of *Capital* is in the last instance a *political* difficulty.

But *Capital* presents another difficulty which has absolutely nothing to do with the first: *Difficulty No. 2*, or the *theoretical* difficulty.

Faced with this difficulty, the same readers divide into two new groups. Those who are used to *theoretical* thought (i.e. the real scientists) do not or should not have any difficulty in reading a *theoretical* book like *Capital*. Those who are not used to practising works of theory (the workers, and many intellectuals who, although they may be 'cultured' are not *theoretically* cultured) must or ought to have great difficulty in reading a book of pure theory like *Capital*.

As the reader will have noted, I have used conditionals (should not . . . should . . .). I have done so in order to stress something even more paradoxical than what I have just discussed: the fact that even individuals without practice in theoretical texts (such as workers) have had less difficulty with *Capital* than individuals disciplined in the practice of pure theory (such as scientists, or very 'cultivated' pseudo-scientists).

This cannot excuse us from saying something about the very special type of difficulty presented by *Capital* as a work of *pure theory*, although we must bear in mind the fundamental fact that it is not the theoretical difficulties but the *political* difficulties which are really determinant in the last instance for every reading of *Capital* and its first volume.

Everyone knows that without a corresponding scientific *theory* there can be no scientific practice, i.e. no practice producing new scientific knowledges. All science therefore depends on its own theory. The fact that this theory changes and is progessively complicated and modified with the development of the science in question makes no difference to this.

Now, what is this theory which is indispensable to every science? It is a *system of basic scientific concepts*. The mere formulation of this simple definition brings out two essential aspects of every scientific theory: (1) the basic concepts, and (2) their system.

These concepts are concepts, i.e. *abstract* notions. First

difficulty of the theory: to get used to the practice of *abstraction*. This apprenticeship, for it really is an appenticeship (comparable with the apprenticeship in any other practice, e.g. as a lock-smith), is primarily provided, in our education system, by mathematics and philosophy. Even in the *Preface* to *Capital* Volume One, Marx warns us that abstraction is not just the existence of theory, but also the method of his analysis. The experimental sciences have the 'microscope', Marxist science has no 'microscope': it has to use abstraction to 'replace' it.

Beware: scientific abstraction is not at all 'abstract', quite the contrary. E.g., when Marx speaks of the total social capital, no one can 'touch it with his hands'; when Marx speaks of the 'total surplus-value', no one can touch it with his hands or count it: and yet these two abstract concepts designate actually existing realities. What makes abstraction scientific is precisely the fact that it designates a concrete reality which certainly exists but which it is impossible to 'touch with one's hands' or 'see with one's eyes'. Every abstract concept therefore provides knowledge of a reality whose existence it reveals: an 'abstract concept' then means a formula which is apparently abstract but really terribly concrete, because of the object it designates. This object is terribly concrete in that it is infinitely more concrete, more effective than the objects one can 'touch with one's hands' or 'see with one's eyes' – and yet one cannot touch it with one's hands or see it with one's eyes. Thus the concept of exchange value, the concept of the total social capital, the concept of socially necessary labour, etc. All this is easy to explain.

The second point: the basic concepts exist in the form of a *system*, and that is what makes them a theory. A theory is indeed a *rigorous* system of basic scientific concepts. In a scientific theory, the basic concepts do not exist in any given order, but in a rigorous order. It is therefore necessary to know this order, and to learn the practice of rigour step by step. Rigour (systematic rigour) is not a fantasy, nor is it a formal luxury, but a vital necessity for all science, for every scientific practice. It is what Marx in his 'Afterword' calls the rigour of the *'method of presentation'* of a scientific theory.

Having said this, we have to know what the object of *Capital* is, in other words, what is the object analysed in *Capital* Volume One. Marx tells us: it is *'the capitalist mode of production and the relations of production and exchange corresponding to that mode'*. This is itself an *abstract* object. Indeed, despite appearances, Marx does not analyse any 'concrete society', not even England which he mentions constantly in Volume One, but the CAPITALIST MODE OF PRODUCTION and nothing else. This object is an abstract one: which means that it is terribly real and that it never *exists* in the pure state, since it only exists in capitalist societies. Simply speaking: in order to be able to analyse these concrete capitalist societies (England, France, Russia, etc.), it is essential to know that they are dominated by that terribly concrete reality, the capitalist mode of production, which is 'invisible' (to the naked eye). 'Invisible', i.e. *abstract*.

Of course, this does not deal with every misunderstanding. We have to be extremely careful to avoid the false difficulties raised by these misunderstandings. For example, we must not imagine that Marx is analysing the concrete situation in England when he discusses it. He only discusses it in order to 'illustrate' his (abstract) theory of the capitalist mode of production.

To sum up: there really is a difficulty in reading *Capital* which is a theoretical difficulty. It lies in the abstract and systematic nature of the basic concepts of the theory or theoretical analysis. It is essential to realize that this is a real difficulty that can only be surmounted by an apprenticeship in scientific abstraction and rigour. It is essential to realize that this apprenticeship is not quickly completed.

Hence a *first* piece of advice to the reader: always keep closely in mind the idea that *Capital* is a work of *theory*, and that its object is the mechanisms of the capitalist mode of production alone.

Hence a *second* piece of advice to the reader: do not look to *Capital* either for a book of 'concrete' history or for a book of 'empirical' political economy, in the sense in which historians and economists understand these terms. Instead, find in it a book of theory analysing the CAPITALIST MODE OF PRODUCTION. History (concrete history) and economics (empirical economics) have other objects.

Hence a *third* piece of advice to the reader. When you encounter a difficulty of a theoretical order in your reading, realize the fact and take the necessary steps. Do not hurry, go back carefully and slowly and do not proceed until you have understood. Take note of the fact that an apprenticeship in theory is indispensable if you are to be able to read a theoretical work. Realize that *you can learn to walk by walking*, on condition that you scrupulously respect the above-mentioned conditions. Realize that you will not learn to walk in theory all at once, suddenly and definitively, but little by little, patiently and humbly. This is the price of success.

Practically, this means that it is impossible to understand Volume One except on condition of re-reading it four or five times in succession, i.e. the time it takes to learn to walk in theory.

The present preface is intended to guide the reader's first steps in the theory.

But before I turn to that, a word is needed on the audience who are going to read *Capital* Volume One.

Of whom is this audience likely to be composed?

1. Proletarians or wage-earners directly employed in the production of material goods.

2. Non-proletarian wage-labourers (from the simple white-collar worker to middle and higher executives, engineers and research workers, teachers, etc.).

3. Urban and rural artisans.

4. Members of the liberal professions.

5. Students at school and university.

Among the proletarians or wage-earners who will read *Capital* Volume One, there will naturally be men and women who have obtained a certain 'idea' of Marxist theory from the practice of the class struggle in their trade-union and political organizations. This idea may be more or less correct, as one passes from the proletarians to the non-proletarian wage-workers : it will not be fundamentally falsified.

Among the other categories who will read *Capital* Volume One, there will naturally be men and women who also have a certain 'idea' of Marxist theory in their heads. For example, academics, and particularly 'historians', 'economists' and a number of ideologists from various disciplines (for, as is well known, in the Human Sciences today, everyone claims to be a 'Marxist').

But nine-tenths of the ideas these intellectuals have in their heads about Marxism are false. These false ideas were expounded even in Marx's own lifetime and they have been tirelessly repeated ever since without any remarkable effort of the imagination. Every bourgeois or petty-bourgeois economist or ideologist[5] for the last hundred years has manu-

5. These are not polemical phrases, but scientific concepts from the pen of Marx himself in *Capital*.

factured and defended these false ideas in order to 'refute' Marxist theory.

These ideas have had no trouble 'winning' a wide audience, since the latter was 'won' to them in advance by its anti-socialist and anti-Marxist ideological prejudices.

This wide audience is primarily composed of intellectuals and not of workers, for, as Engels said, even when proletarians have not grasped the most abstract demonstrations in *Capital*, they do not allow themselves to be 'caught out'.

On the contrary, even the most generously 'revolutionary' intellectuals and students do allow themselves to be 'caught out' in one direction or another, since they are massively subject to the prejudices of petty-bourgeois ideology without the counterpoise of a direct experience of exploitation.

In this preface, I am therefore obliged to take conjointly into account:

1. the two orders of difficulties which I have already signalled (Difficulty No. 1 – political, Difficulty No. 2 – theoretical);

2. the distribution of the audience into two essential groups: the wage-labouring audience on the one hand, the intellectual audience on the other, it being understood that these two groups intersect at one of their boundaries (certain wage-earners are at the same time 'intellectual workers');

3. the existence on the ideological market of supposedly 'scientific' refutations of *Capital* which affect the various parts of this audience more or less profoundly according to their class origins.

Allowing for all these facts, my preface will take the following form:

Point I: Advice to the reader with the aim of avoiding the toughest of these difficulties for the time being. This point can be quickly and clearly dealt with. I hope that proletarians will read it because I have written it for them especially, although it is valid for everybody.

Point II: Suggestions as to the nature of the theoretical difficulties in *Capital* Volume One which provide a pretext for all the refutations of Marxist theory.

This point will inevitably be much more arduous, given the nature of the theoretical difficulties in question, and the arguments of the 'refutations' of Marxist theory which are erected out of these difficulties.

POINT I

The greatest difficulties, theoretical or otherwise, which are obstacles to an easy reading of *Capital* Volume One are unfortunately (or fortunately) concentrated *at the very beginning* of Volume One, to be precise, in its first Part, which deals with 'Commodities and Money'.

I therefore give the following advice: put THE WHOLE OF PART ONE ASIDE FOR THE TIME BEING and BEGIN YOUR READING WITH PART TWO: 'The Transformation of Money into Capital'.

In my opinion it is impossible to begin (even to begin) to understand Part I until you have read and re-read the whole of Volume One, *starting with Part II*.

This advice is more than advice: it is a recommendation that, notwithstanding all the respect I owe my readers, I am prepared to present as an *imperative*.

Everyone can try it out in practice for himself.

If you begin Volume One at the beginning, i.e. with Part I, either you do not understand it, and give up; or you think you understand it, but that is even more serious, for there is every chance that you will have understood something quite different from what there was to be understood.

From Part II (The Transformation of Money into Capital) on, things are luminous. You go straight into the heart of Volume One.

This heart is the theory of *surplus-value*, which proletarians will understand without any difficulty, because it is quite simply the scientific theory of something they experience every day: *class exploitation.*

It is immediately followed by two very dense but very clear sections which are decisive for the class struggle *even today*: Parts III and IV. They deal with the two basic *forms* of *surplus-value* available to the capitalist class for it to push the exploitation of the working class to a maximum: what Marx calls *absolute* surplus-value (Part III) and *relative* surplus-value (Part IV).

Absolute surplus-value (Part III) concerns the length of the working day. Marx explains that the capitalist class inexorably presses for the lengthening of the working day and that the more than century-old workers' class struggle has as its aim a *reduction* of the working day by struggling AGAINST that lengthening.

The historical stages of that struggle are well known: the twelve-hour day, the ten-hour day, then the eight-hour day, and finally, under the Popular Front, the forty-hour week.

Every proletarian knows from experience what Marx demonstrates in Part III: the irresistible tendency of the capitalist system to increase exploitation as much as possible by lengthening the working day (or the working week). This result is obtained either despite existing legislation (the forty-hour week was never really enforced) or by means of existing legislation (e.g., 'overtime'). Overtime seems to 'cost the capitalists a greal deal' since they pay time-and-a quarter, time-and-a-half or even double time as compared with normal rates. But in reality it is to their advantage since it makes it possible to run the 'machines', which have a shorter life because of the rapidity of technological progress, twenty-four hours a day. In other words, overtime enables the capitalists to draw the maximum profit from 'productivity'. Marx showed that the capitalist class has never paid and will never pay the workers overtime rates to please them, or to allow them to supplement their incomes at the cost of their health, but only in order to exploit them more.

Relative surplus-value (Part IV), whose existence can be glimpsed in what I have just said about overtime, is undoubtedly the number-one form of contemporary exploitation. It is much more subtle because less directly visible than the lengthening of the working day. However, proletarians react instinctively if not against it, at least, as we shall see, against its effects.

Relative surplus-value deals in fact with the intensification of the mechanization of (industrial and agricultural) production, and thus with the resulting rise in productivity. At present it tends towards automation. To produce the maximum of commodities at the lowest price in order to get the highest profit, such is the irresistible tendency of capitalism. Naturally, it goes hand in hand with an increasing exploitation of labour power.

There is a tendency to talk about a 'mutation' or 'revolution' in contemporary technology. In reality, Marx claimed as early as the *Manifesto* and proved in *Capital* that the capitalist mode of production is characterized by its 'constantly revolutionizing the means of production', above all, the instruments of production (technology). What has happened in the last ten to fifteen years is described in grandiose statements as 'unprecedented', and it is true that in the last few years things have gone quicker than before. But this is merely a difference of *degree*, not a difference of kind. The whole history of capitalism is the history of a fantastic growth of productivity, through the development of technology.

The result at the moment, as in the past, is the introduction of more and more perfected machines into the labour process – making it possible to produce the same quantity of products as before in one half, one third or one quarter of the time – i.e. a manifest growth in productivity. But correlatively, the result is certain effects of the aggravation of the exploitation of labour power (speed-up, the elimination of blue- and white-collar jobs) not only for proletarians but also for non-proletarian wage-labourers, including certain technicians and executives, even in the higher grades, who can no longer 'keep up' with technical progress and therefore have no more market value, hence the subsequent unemployment.

Marx deals with all these things with great rigour and precision in Part IV (Relative Surplus-Value).

He dismantles the mechanisms of exploitation deriving from the growth of productivity in its concrete forms. He shows thereby that *the growth of productivity is never spontaneously to the advantage of the working class*, quite the contrary, since it is precisely introduced to increase its exploitation. Marx thus proves irrefutably that the working class cannot hope to gain from the modern growth of productivity before it has overthrown capitalism and seized State power in a socialist revolution. He proves that from here to the revolutionary seizure of power which opens the road to socialism, the working class can have no other objective, and hence no other resource, than to struggle *against* the effects of exploitation produced by the growth of productivity, in order to *limit* these effects (struggle *against* speed-up, *against* arbitrary productivity bonuses, *against* overtime, *against* redundancies, *against* 'automation unemployment'). An essentially *defensive*, not an offensive struggle.

I then advise the reader who has reached the end of Part IV to leave Part V (The Production of Absolute and Relative Surplus-Value) for the moment, and to move directly on to Part VI, on Wages, which is perfectly clear.

Here, too, proletarians are literally *at home* since, besides examining the bourgeois mystification which declares that the worker's 'labour' is 'paid at its value', Marx looks at the different *forms* of wages: time-wages first of all, then piece-rates, i.e. the different *traps* the bourgeoisie sets for the workers' consciousness, hoping to destroy in it all an organized class's will to struggle. Here proletarians will recognize that their class struggle cannot but *be opposed in an antagonistic way to the tendency for capitalist exploitation to increase.*

Here, on the plane of wages, or as cabinet ministers and their economists say, on the plane of the 'standard of living' or of 'income' respectively, they will recognize that the economic class struggle of the proletarians and other wage-earners can have only one meaning: a *defensive* struggle against the objective tendency of the capitalist system to increase exploitation in all its forms.

I say a defensive struggle and therefore a struggle *against* the fall in wages. Of course, any struggle *against* a fall in wages is at the same time also a struggle *for* a rise in the existing wages. But to speak only of a struggle *for* a rise would be to describe the effect of the struggle while running the risk of masking its cause and its objective. As capitalism tends inexorably to reduce wages, the struggle for wage increases is therefore, in principle, *a defensive struggle against the tendency of capitalism to reduce wages.*

It is therefore perfectly clear, as Marx emphasizes in

Part VI, that the question of wages certainly cannot be *settled 'by itself' by 'sharing out' the 'gains' from even a spectacular growth in productivity among the proletarians and other labourers.* The question of wages is a question of class struggle. It is not settled 'by itself', but by class struggle: above all by the different forms of strike, eventually leading to general strike.

Such a general strike is purely economic and therefore defensive ('a defence of the material and moral interests of the labourers', a struggle *against* the double capitalist tendency to increase labour-time and reduce wages) or takes a political and therefore offensive form (struggle for the conquest of State power, socialist revolution and the construction of socialism); all those who know the distinctions made by Marx, Engels and Lenin know the difference between the political class struggle and the economic class struggle.

The economic (trade-union) class struggle remains a defensive one because it is economic (*against* the two great tendencies of capitalism). The political class struggle is offensive because it is political (*for* the seizure of power by the working class and its allies).

These two struggles must be carefully distinguished; although in reality they always encroach upon one another: more or less, according to the conjuncture.

One thing is certain, and the analysis which Marx makes of the economic class struggles in England in Volume One shows it: a class struggle which is *deliberately restricted* to the domain of economic struggle alone has always remained and will always remain a defensive one, i.e. one with no hope of ever overthrowing the capitalist regime. This is the great temptation of the reformists, Fabians, and trade-unionists whom Marx discusses, and in a general way of the

Social-Democratic tradition of the Second International. Only a political struggle can 'reverse steam' and go beyond these limits, thereby ceasing to be a defensive struggle and becoming an offensive one. This conclusion is legible between the lines in *Capital*, and it can be read in so many words in the political texts of Marx himself, of Engels and of Lenin. It has been the number-one question of the International Workers' Movement since it 'fused' with Marxist theory.

Readers can then go on to Part VII (The Accumulation of Capital), which is very clear. There Marx explains that it is the tendency of capitalism to reproduce and expand the very basis of capital, since this tendency is the transformation into capital of the surplus-value extorted from the proletariat, and therefore that capital constantly 'snowballs', constantly extorting more surplus labour (surplus-value) from the proletarians. And Marx shows this in a magnificent concrete 'illustration': that of England from 1846 to 1866.

As for Part VIII (The So-called Primitive Accumulation), which brings Volume One to an end, it contains the second of Marx's greatest discoveries. The first was the discovery of 'surplus-value'. The second is the discovery of the incredible means used to achieve the 'primitive accumulation' thanks to which capitalism was 'born' and grew in Western societies, helped also by the existence of a mass of 'free labourers' (i.e. labourers stripped of means of labour) and technological discoveries. This means was the most brutal violence: the thefts and massacres which cleared capitalism's royal road into human history. This last chapter contains a prodigious wealth which has not yet been exploited: in particular the thesis (which we shall have to develop) that capitalism has always used and, in the 'margins' of its metropolitan existence – i.e. in the colonial and ex-colonial countries – is still using well into the twentieth century, *the most brutally violent means.*

I therefore urge on the reader the following method of reading:

1. Leave Part I (Commodities and Money) deliberately on one side in a first reading.

2. Begin reading Volume One with its Part II (The Transformation of Money into Capital).

3. Read carefully Parts II, III (The Production of Absolute Surplus-Value) and IV (The Production of Relative Surplus-Value).

4. Leave Part V (The Production of Relative and Absolute Surplus-Value) on one side.

5. Read carefully Parts VI (Wages), VII (The Accumulation of Capital) and VIII (The So-called Primitive Accumulation).

6. Finally, begin to read Part I (Commodities and Money) with infinite caution, knowing that it will always be extremely difficult to understand, even after several readings of the other Parts, without the help of a certain number of deeper explanations.

I guarantee that those readers who are prepared to observe this order of reading scrupulously, remembering what I have said about the political and theoretical difficulties of every reading of *Capital*, will not regret it.

POINT II

I now come to the theoretical difficulties which are obstacles to a quick reading, and even at certain points even to a very careful reading of *Capital* Volume One.

Let me remind the reader that it is by building on these difficulties that bourgeois ideology attempts to convince itself – but does it really succeed? – that it has long since 'refuted' Marx's theory.

The first difficulty is of a very general kind. It derives from the simple fact that Volume One is only the *first* volume in a book containing *four*.

I say four. Most people know about Volumes One, Two and Three, but even those who had read them usually ignore Volume Four, even supposing that they suspect its existence.

The 'mystery' of Volume Four is only a mystery for those who think Marx was one of a number of 'historians', the author of a *History of Economic Doctrines*, since this is the aberrant title that Molitor has given to his translation,[6] if that word is applicable, of a certain profoundly theoretical work really called *Theories of Surplus-Value*.

Certainly *Capital* Volume One is the only one Marx published in his lifetime, Volumes Two and Three having been published after his death in 1883 by Engels, and Volume Four by Kautsky.[7] In 1886, in his preface to the English edition, Engels could say that Volume One 'is in a great measure a whole in itself'. Indeed, when the following volumes were not available, it had to 'rank as an independent work'.

This is not the case today. All four volumes are available, in German,[8] and in French.[9] To those who read German, I suggest that they have much to gain by referring constantly to the German text to check the French translations, not just of Volume Four (which is riddled with serious errors),

6. Karl Marx, *Histoire des doctrines économiques*, 8 volumes, Éditions Costes, Paris, 1924–36.
7. Volume Two in 1885, Volume Three in 1894, Volume Four in 1905.
8. Dietz Verlag, Berlin.
9. Éditions Sociales, Paris, for Volumes One to Three, Éditions Costes for Volume Four [in English, Progress Publishers, Moscow, for Volumes One to Three and *Theories of Surplus-Value* Parts I and II – Part III forthcoming].

but also of Volumes Two and Three (certain terminological difficulties have not always been solved) and even of Volume One, translated by Roy, in a version which Marx personally completely revised, correcting and even appreciably expanding certain passages. For Marx, who was uncertain of the theoretical capacities of his French readers,[10] sometimes dangerously compromised the precision of the original conceptual expressions.[11]

Knowledge of the other three Volumes makes it possible to remove a certain number of the very serious theoretical difficulties of Volume One, especially those concentrated in the notorious Part I (Commodities and Money) around the famous 'labour theory of value'.

In the grip of a Hegelian conception of science (for Hegel, all science is philosophical and therefore every true science *has to found its own beginnings*), Marx then thought that the principle that 'every beginning is difficult . . . holds in all sciences'. In fact, Volume One Part I follows a method of presentation whose difficulty largely derives from this Hegelian prejudice. Moreover, Marx redrafted this beginning a dozen times before giving it its 'definitive' form – as if he was struggling with a difficulty which was not just one of presentation – and with good reason.

Let me very briefly give the principles of a solution.

Marx's 'labour theory of value' which all bourgeois 'economists' and ideologists have used against him in their scornful condemnations, is intelligible, but only as a special

10. See the text of Marx's letter to La Châtre, his French publisher, in *Capital*, Vol. I, p. 21.
11. [The English translation of Volume One, by Moore and Aveling, was checked and approved by Engels. All the other translations in the Progress Publishers editions, including that of Volume Four, were done under the supervision of the Marx–Engels Institute, Moscow. Despite this, however, many of Althusser's strictures could be applied to the English translations too.]

case of a theory which Marx and Engels called the '*law of value*' or the law of the distribution of the available labour power between the various branches of production, a distribution indispensable to the *reproduction* of the conditions of production. 'Every child' could understand it, says Marx in 1868, in terms which thus deny the inevitable 'difficult beginning' of every science. On the nature of this law I refer the reader to Marx's letters to Kugelmann on 6 March and 11 July 1868, among other texts.[12]

The 'labour theory of value' is not the only point which causes difficulty in Volume One. We must of course mention the theory of *surplus-value*, the *bête noire* of bourgeois economists and ideologists who attack it as 'metaphysical', 'Aristotelian', 'non-operational', etc. Now this theory of surplus-value, too, is intelligible only as a special case of a wider theory: the theory of *surplus labour*.

Surplus labour exists in every 'society'. In classless societies, once the portion necessary for the reproduction of the conditions of production has been set aside, it is *shared* between the members of the 'community' (the primitive or communist community). In class societies, once the portion necessary for the reproduction of the conditions of production has been set aside, it is *extorted* from the exploited classes by the ruling classes. In capitalist class society, in which labour power becomes a *commodity* for the first time in history, the extorted surplus labour takes the form of *surplus-value*.

Here again, I shall go no further: I am content to suggest the principles of the solution whose proof would demand detailed argument.

Volume One contains further theoretical difficulties, linked to the preceding ones or to other problems.

12. *Selected Correspondence*, Progress Publishers, Moscow, 1955, pp. 199 and 208.

For example, the theory of the distinction which has to be introduced between *value* and the *value-form*; for example, the theory of the *socially necessary* quantity of labour; for example, the theory of *simple* and *compound* labour; for example, the theory of *social needs*, etc. For example, the theory of the *organic composition of capital.* For example, the famous theory of the '*fetishism*' of commodities and its later generalization.

All these questions – and many others – constitute real, objective difficulties to which Volume One gives either provisional or partial solutions. Why this incompleteness?

We must realize that when Marx published Volume One of *Capital,* he had already written Volume Two and part of Volume Three (the latter in note form). At any rate, as his correspondence with Engels proves,[13] he had it 'all in his head', at least *in principle*. But there was no question of Marx being materially able to put it 'all on paper' in the first volume of a work which was to contain four. In addition, if Marx did have it 'all in his head', he did not yet have answers to all the questions he had in his head – and at certain points this can be detected in Volume One. It is no accident that it was only in 1868, i.e. a year after the publication of Volume One, that Marx wrote that it was within the reach of 'every child' to understand the 'law of value' on which depends an understanding of Part I.

The reader of Volume One must therefore convince himself of one thing, which is completely comprehensible once he is prepared to consider the fact that Marx was advancing for the first time in the history of human knowledge in a virgin continent: Volume One contains certain solutions to problems which were only to be posed in Volumes Two, Three and Four – and certain problems

13. See *Selected Correspondence,* op. cit.

whose solutions were only to be demonstrated in Volumes
Two, Three and Four.

Essentially, most of the objective difficulties of Volume
One derive from this 'suspended', or if you like, 'antici-
patory' character. Hence it is essential to realize this and to
draw the conclusions: i.e. to read Volume One taking
Volumes Two, Three and Four into account.

Nevertheless, there is also a second kind of difficulty
constituting a real obstacle to a reading of Volume One.
These difficulties no longer derive from the fact that *Capital*
has four volumes, but from survivals in Marx's language
and even in his thought of the influence of Hegel's thought.

As the reader may know, I have previously attempted to
defend the idea that Marx's thought is basically different
from that of Hegel, and that there was therefore a true
break or rupture, if you prefer, between Marx and Hegel.[14]
The further I go, the more I think this thesis is correct.
However, I must admit that I have given a much too abrupt
idea of this thesis in advancing the idea that it was possible
to locate this rupture in 1845 (the *Theses on Feuerbach, The
German Ideology*). Something decisive really does begin in
1845, but Marx needed a very long period of revolutionary
work before he managed to register the rupture he had made
with Hegel's thought in really new concepts. The famous
Preface of 1859 (to *A Contribution to the Critique of Political
Economy*) is still profoundly Hegelian-evolutionist. The
'*Grundrisse*', which date from the years 1857–59, are themselves profoundly marked by Hegel's thought, for in 1858
Marx had re-read the *Great Logic* with amazement.

When *Capital* Volume One appeared (1867), traces of
the Hegelian influence still remained. Only later did they
disappear *completely*: the *Critique of the Gotha Programme*

14. *For Marx*, Vintage Books, New York, 1970.

(1875)[15] as well as the *Marginal Notes on Wagner's 'Lehrbuch der politischen Ökonomie'* (1882)[16] are *totally and definitively exempt* from *any* trace of Hegelian influence.

It is therefore of the first importance for us to know *where Marx started*: he began with the neo-Hegelianism which was a retreat from Hegel to Kant and Fichte, then with pure Feuerbachianism, then with Feuerbachianism with a Hegelian injection (the *1844 Manuscripts*)[17] before rediscovering Hegel in 1858.

It is also important to know *where he was going*. The *tendency* of his thought drove him irresistibly to the *radical* abandonment of every shade of Hegelian influence, as can be seen from the 1875 *Critique of the Gotha Programme* and the 1882 *Notes on Wagner*. While remorselessly abandoning all Hegel's influence, Marx continued to recognize an important debt to him: the fact that he was the first to conceive of history as a 'process without a subject'.

By taking this tendency into account we can appreciate the traces of Hegelian influence which remain in Volume One as survivals on the way to supersession.

I have already noted these traces in the typically Hegelian problem of the 'difficult beginning' to every science, whose striking manifestion is Part I of Volume One. This Hegelian influence can be located very precisely in the *vocabulary* Marx uses in Part I: in the fact that he speaks of two *completely* different things, the social usefulness of products on the one hand and the exchange value of the same products on the other, in terms which in fact have *a word in common*, the word 'value': on the one hand use-*value*, and on the other exchange *value*. Marx pillories a man named Wagner

15. *Selected Works*, International Publishers, New York, 1968, pp. 315–35.
16. No English translation.
17. *Economic and Philosophical Manuscripts of 1844*, International Publishers, New York, 1964.

(that *vir obscurus*) with his customary vigour in the *Marginal Notes* of 1882, because Wagner seems to believe that since Marx uses the same word, *value*, in both cases, use-value and exchange value are the result of a (Hegelian) division of the concept of 'value'. The fact is that Marx had not taken the precaution of eliminating the word *value* from the expression 'use-value' and of speaking as he should have done simply of the *social usefulness* of the *products*. That is why in 1873, in the *Afterword* to the second German edition of *Capital*, we find Marx retreating from his earlier positions and recognizing that he had even dared to 'coquett' (*kokettieren*) 'with the modes of expression peculiar' to Hegel 'in the chapter on the theory of value' (precisely, Part I). We ought to draw the conclusions from this, which means ultimately that we ought to *rewrite Part I of Capital*, so that it becomes a 'beginning' which is no longer at all 'difficult', but rather simple and easy.

The same Hegelian influence comes to light in the imprudent formulation in Chapter 32 of Volume One Part VIII, where Marx, discussing the 'expropriation of the expropriators', declares, '*It is the negation of the negation*'. Imprudent, since its ravages have not yet come to an end, despite the fact that Stalin was right, for once, to suppress 'the negation of the negation' from the laws of the dialectic, it must be said to the advantage of other, even more serious errors.

A last trace of Hegelian influence, this time a flagrant and extremely harmful one (since all the theoreticians of 'reification' and 'alienation' have found in it the 'foundation' for their idealist interpretations of Marx's thought): the theory of *fetishism* (*The Fetishism of Commodities and the Secret Thereof*, Part I, Chapter 1, Section 4).

The reader will realize that I cannot go into these different points, each of which demands a whole demonstration to

itself. Nevertheless, I have signalled them, for, along with
the very ambiguous and (alas!) famous Preface to *A Contribution to the Critique of Political Economy* (1859), the
Hegelianism and evolutionism (evolutionism being a poor
man's Hegelianism) in which they are steeped have made
ravages in the history of the Marxist Workers' Movement.
I note that Lenin did not give in to the influence of these
Hegelian-evolutionist pages *for a single moment*, for otherwise he could not have fought the betrayal of the Second
International, built up the Bolshevik Party, conquered State
power at the head of the mass of the Russian people in
order to install the dictatorship of the proletariat, or begun
the construction of socialism.

I note also that, unfortunately for the same International
Communist Movement, Stalin made the 1859 Preface *his
reference text*, as can be observed in the chapter of the
History of the Russian Communist Party (*Bolshevik*) entitled
Dialectical Materialism and Historical Materialism (1938)
which undoubtedly explains many of the things called by a
name which is not at all Marxist, the 'period of the cult of
personality'. I shall return to this question elsewhere.

Let me add one further comment, to forestall the possibility of a very serious misunderstanding for the reader of
Volume One, one which no longer has anything to do with
the difficulties which I have just raised, but relates to the
necessity of reading Marx's text *very closely*.

This misunderstanding concerns the object which is in
question from the beginning of Part II of Volume One
(The Transformation of Money into Capital). In fact,
Marx there discusses the organic composition of capital,
saying that in capitalist production there is in every
given capital a fraction (say 40 per cent) which constitutes
the constant capital (raw material, buildings, machines,
tools) and another fraction (in this case 60 per cent) which

labour power). The constant capital is so called because it remains constant in the process of capitalist production: it produces no new value, so it remains constant. The variable capital is called variable because it produces a new value, higher than its former value, by the action of the extortion of surplus-value (which takes place in the use of labour power).

Now, the vast majority of readers, including of course the 'economists' who are, if I may say so, destined to this 'oversight' by their professional distortion as technicians of bourgeois political economy, believe that when he discusses the organic composition of capital, Marx is constructing a theory of the firm, or, to use Marxist terms, a theory of the unit of production. However, Marx says quite the opposite: he always discusses the composition of the *total* social capital, but in the form of an apparently concrete example for which he *gives figures* (e.g. out of 100 million, constant capital = 40 millions – 40 per cent – and variable capital = 60 millions – 60 per cent). In this *arithmetical* example, Marx is thus not talking about one firm or another, but of a 'fraction of the total capital'. For the convenience of the reader and in order to 'crystallize his ideas', he argues around a 'concrete' (i.e. arithmetical) example, but this concrete example simply provides him with an example so that he can talk about the *total* social capital.

In this perspective, let me signal the fact that nowhere in *Capital* is there any theory of the capitalist unit of production or of the capitalist unit of consumption. On these two points, Marx's theory thus has still to be complemented.

I also note the *political* importance of this confusion, which was definitively dealt with by Lenin in his theory of Imperialism.[18] As we know, Marx planned to discuss the constitutes the variable capital (the costs of purchasing

18. *Imperialism, the Highest Stage of Capitalism,* in *Selected Works,* op. cit.

'world market' in *Capital*, i.e. the tendential expansion of the capitalist relations of production throughout the world. This 'tendency' found its final form in Imperialism. It is very important to grasp the decisive political importance of this fact, which Marx and the First International saw very clearly.

In fact, if capitalist exploitation (the extortion of surplus-value) exists *in* the capitalist firms where wage-workers are employed (and the workers are its victims and therefore its direct witnesses), this *local* exploitation only exists as a simple part of a *generalized* system of exploitation which steadily expands from the great urban industrial enterprises to agricultural capitalist enterprises, then to the complex forms of the other sectors (urban and rural artisanat: 'one-family agricultural' units, white-collar workers and officials, etc.), not only in *one* capitalist country, but in the *ensemble* of capitalist countries, and eventually in *all the rest of the world* (by means of *direct* colonial exploitation based on military occupation: colonialism; then *indirect* colonial exploitation, without military occupation: neo-colonialism).

There is in fact, therefore, a real capitalist International, which has been an Imperialist International since the end of the nineteenth century, to which the Workers' Movement and its great leaders (Marx, then Lenin) responded with a Workers' International (the First, Second, and Third Internationals). Working-class militants recognize this fact in their practice of Proletarian Internationalism. Concretely this means that they know very well:

1. that they are directly exploited in the capitalist firm (unit of production) in which they work;

2. that they cannot conduct the struggle solely at the level of their own firm, but must also conduct it at the level of their national production (engineering, building and

transport trade-union federations, etc.), then at the level of the national set of different branches of production (e.g. in the *Confédération Générale de Travail* – the General Confederation of Labour – in France), and finally at the world level (e.g. the World Federation of Trade Unions).

This where the economic class struggle is concerned.

The same is naturally the case, despite the disappearance of a formal International, where the political class struggle is concerned. That is why Volume One must be read *in the light* not only of the *Communist Manifesto* ('Workers *of all countries* unite!'), but also of the Statutes of the First, Second and Third Internationals, and of course, *in the light* of the Leninist theory of imperialism.

To say this is not at all to *leave* Volume One of *Capital* to make 'political propaganda' with respect to a book which, it would seem, deals only with 'political economy'. Quite the contrary, it is to take seriously the fact that Marx has opened to scientific knowledge and to men's conscious practice a new continent, the Continent of History, by an amazing discovery, and that, like the discovery of every new science, this discovery extends into the history of this science and into the political practice of the men who have recognized themselves in it. Marx was not able to write the projected chapter of *Capital* with the title 'The World Market' as a foundation for proletarian Internationalism, in response to the capitalist, later imperialist International, but the First International, which Marx founded in 1864, had already begun to write this same chapter in the facts, three years before the appeatance of *Capital* Volume One, and Lenin wrote the continuation of it not only in his book *Imperialism, the Highest Stage of Capitalism*, but also in the foundation of the Third International (1919).

All this is, of course, if not incomprehensible, at least

very hard to understand if one is an 'economist' or even a 'historian', *a fortiori* if one is a mere 'ideologist' of the bourgeoisie. On the contrary, it is all very easy to understand if one is a proletarian, i.e. a wage-labourer 'employed' in capitalist production (urban or agricultural).

Why this difficulty? Why this relative ease? I believe that I have been able to explain it by following some of Marx's own texts and the clarifications that Lenin provides in his commentaries on Marx's *Capital* in the first volumes of his *Collected Works*. It is because bourgeois and petty-bourgeois intellectuals have a bourgeois (or petty-bourgeois) 'class instinct', whereas proletarians have a proletarian class instinct. The former, blinded by bourgeois ideology which does everything it can to cover up class exploitation, cannot *see* capitalist exploitation. The latter, on the contrary, despite the terrible weight of bourgeois and petty-bourgeois ideology they carry, cannot *fail to see* this exploitation, since it constitutes their daily life.

To understand *Capital*, and therefore its first volume, it is necessary to take up 'proletarian class positions', i.e. to adopt the only viewpoint which makes *visible* the reality of the exploitation of wage labour power, which constitutes the whole of capitalism.

This is, proportionately speaking, on condition that they struggle against the influence of the burden of bourgeois and petty-bourgeois ideology that they carry, relatively easy for workers. As 'by nature' they have a 'class instinct' formed by the harsh school of daily exploitation, all they need is a supplementary political and theoretical education in order to understand objectively what they feel subjectively, instinctively. *Capital* gives them this supplementary theoretical education in the form of objective explanations and proofs, which helps them to move from a proletarian class instinct to an (objective) proletarian class position.

But it is extremely difficult for specialists and other bourgeois and petty-bourgeois 'intellectuals' (including students). For a mere *education* of their consciousness is not enough, nor a mere reading of *Capital*. They must also make a real *rupture*, a real *revolution* in their consciousness, in order to move from their necessarily bourgeois or petty-bourgeois class instinct to proletarian class positions. It is extremely difficult, but not absolutely impossible. The proof: Marx himself, who was the scion of a good liberal bourgeoisie (his father was a lawyer), and Engels, who came from the big capitalist bourgeoisie and was himself a capitalist in Manchester for twenty years. Marx's whole intellectual history can and must be understood in this way: as a long, difficult and painful rupture by which he moved from his petty-bourgeois class instinct to proletarian class positions, to whose definitions he contributed decisively in *Capital*.

This is an example which can and must be meditated upon, bearing in mind other illustrious examples: above all Lenin, the son or an enlightened petty bourgeois (a progressive teacher), who became the leader of the October Revolution and the world proletariat, in the stage of Imperialism, the supreme, i.e. the last stage of capitalism.[19]

March 1969

---

19. Engels gave a brilliant summary of *Capital* in an article which appeared in 1868 in the Leipzig *Demokratisches Wochenblatt*. An English translation can be found in Friedrich Engels, *On Marx's Capital*, Progress Publishers, Moscow, 1956, pp. 13–20.

THE RUDIMENTS OF A CRITICAL BIBLIOGRAPHY[20]

I propose to distinguish between:

I. *Texts earlier than* Capital *Volume One* (1867) which make it easier to understand both the investigatory works of Marx which led up to *Capital* and *Capital* itself.

1. *The Communist Manifesto* (1847).

2. *The Poverty of Philosophy* (1847): a critique of Proudhon.

3. *Wage Labour and Capital* (1848): lectures to a working-class audience on two key concepts of the theory of the capitalist mode of production.

After 1850, when the proletarian risings throughout Europe had been crushed, Marx withdrew to London and decided to 'begin again at the beginning' in political economy, with which up to that time he only had an indirect and superficial acquaintance. Strenuous work in libraries on the economists, the Factory Inspectors' reports, and all the documentation available (cf. his letters in this period in *Selected Correspondence*).

4. The '*Grundrisse*', a collection of preparatory manuscripts for *A Contribution to the Critique of Political Economy*, which appeared in 1859. Only part of these texts went into *A Contribution*. The remarkable '*Introduction*' remained unpublished. In many places in the *Grundrisse* (published in French translation by Éditions Anthropos under the unfortunate title '*Fondements* [foundations] de la critique de l'économie politique')[21] a strong Hegelian influence can be detected, combined with whiffs of Feuerbachian humanism.

---

20. Unless otherwise stated, the works referred to exist in translations published by International Publishers.

21. One section has been translated under the title *Pre-Capitalist Economic Formations*, International Publishers, New York, 1965.

It can be predicted with some certainty that, along with *The German Ideology*, the *Grundrisse* will provide all the dubious quotations needed by idealist interpretations of Marxist theory.

5. *A Contribution to the Critique of Political Economy* (1859), the crucial part of which (the theory of money) was incorporated in Part I of *Capital* Volume One. The famous *Preface* is unfortunately deeply marked by a Hegelian-evolutionist conception which disappears 99 per cent in *Capital* and completely in Marx's later texts.

6. *Wages, Price and Profits* (1865). Lectures given by Marx to a working-class audience. A very important text in which the concepts of *Capital* are already perfectly formed.

7. Correspondence on *Capital* before 1867, collected under the title *Lettres sur le Capital*.[22] Here it is possible to see directly how Marx learnt from that excellent 'capitalist' Engels about the labour process, the instruments of labour (machines), the organic composition of capital in a firm, the turnover of the different fractions of capital, etc. It is possible to see Marx submit his hypotheses and results to Engels, ask him questions, take note of his answers. It is possible to discover that Marx already had the essentials of *Capital* in his head well before 1867, not just Volume One, but also Volumes Two and Three, since he talks at length about the theory of ground rent and the tendency for the rate of profit to fall (which only appeared in Volume Three, published by Engels after his death).

II. *Texts later than Capital*, either by Marx himself or by other great writers (Engels, Lenin, etc.).

These texts are doubly useful: they cast light on a number

22. No English equivalent, but many of these letters are to be found in *Selected Correspondence*, Progress Publishers, Moscow, 1955.

of difficult points in *Capital*, or greatly facilitate reading it; and they extend the investigations of the theory founded by Marx, demonstrating its fruitfulness in concrete applications.

8. The Second Part of Engels's *Anti-Dühring* (1877) which gives a very clear summary of the crucial theses of Volume One.

9. Marx's *Critique of the Gotha Programme* (1875). Mere '*Randglossen*' (marginal notes) in Marx's hand on the joint draft Programme on which the (Marxist) 'Social Democratic Workers' Party' and the (Lassallean) 'General Association of German Workers' agreed to the organic unification of their two organizations in the German Social-Democratic Party. No notice was taken of the criticism of Marx and Engels, who thought of publicly dissociating themselves from the new organization, but decided against it since the 'bourgeoisie saw in the programme what was not there'. Marx's mere notes are invaluable. They discuss the principles which ought to have guided any policy of unification, revolution and socialism, four years after the Paris Commune. In them there is the starting-point for a theory of Law: Law is always bourgeois. It is not the 'collective ownership' (legal notion) 'of the means of production', but their 'collective appropriation' which defines the socialist mode of production. The fundamental thesis: legal relations and the relations of production must not be confused.

The history of the misadventures of the *Critique* is instructive. Barred from publication by the leadership of the Social-Democratic Party, it could only appear . . . sixteen years later, thanks to Engels, who had to trick this same leadership and only obtained his objective by the skin of his teeth. The leadership of the Social-Democratic Party was radically opposed to the publication of Marx's critical notes 'so as not to damage our unity with our Lassallean comrades'. . . .

10. Marx's *Marginal Notes on Wagner's 'Lehrbuch der politischen Ökonomie'* (1882). The last text written by Marx, slightly abridged in the French translation published by Éditions Sociales (*Le Capital*, t. III, pp. 241–53).[23] It reveals irrefutably the direction in which Marx's thought tended: no longer the shadow of a trace of Feuerbachian-humanist or Hegelian influence.

11. The Prefaces and articles by Engels collected together into the volume *On Marx's Capital* (Progress Publishers, Moscow). First-rate analyses, very clear, but, as sometimes happens with Engels who had touches of theoretical genius, marred by a few weaknesses (e.g. the thesis that the 'law of value' only ceased to apply . . . in the fourteenth century).

12. Lenin's *What the 'Friends of the People' Are* (Progress Publishers, Moscow) (1894: Lenin was twenty-four years old). A critique of the idealist-humanist ideology of the Populists. An exposition of the epistemological principles of Marx's scientific discovery. A categorical affirmation that Marx's dialectic has nothing to do with that of Hegel.

13. Lenin's *The Development of Capitalism in Russia* (1899: Lenin was twenty-nine years old). The only work of scientific sociology in the world, which all sociologists should study with care. An application of the theory of the feudal and capitalist modes of production to the Russian social formation at the end of the nineteenth century, where capitalist relations of production and exchange were extending through the countryside, supplanting feudal relations of production. This work summarizes the essentials of the numerous studies that Lenin devoted to the basic theses of *Capital* Volume Two in texts of a gripping clarity and rigour, between 1894 and 1899, in his critique of the Populist and 'romantic' 'economists'. A text to be related to

23. No English translation.

Kautsky's *Agrarian Question* (1903)[24] of which Lenin had a high opinion, and above all to 'New Data on the Laws Governing the Development of Capitalism in Agriculture' (1915: Vol. 22 of the English edition of the *Collected Works*), where Lenin deals with the 'paradox' of the advanced capitalist development of small agricultural enterprises in the USA alongside big capitalist enterprises. French 'specialists' in 'agrarian questions' have every interest in reading this very actual text closely, and learning from it how official statistics should be 'handled'.

14. Lenin's *Marxism and Revisionism* (1908).[25]

15. Lenin's *Three Sources and Three Component Parts of Marxism* (1913).

16. Lenin's *The Historical Destiny of the Doctrine of Karl Marx* (1913).

17. Lenin's *Imperialism the Highest Stage of Capitalism* (1916).

18. Lenin's *State and Revolution* (1917).

I shall finish this little critical bibliography here.

There are a large number of essays, usually critical or highly critical, devoted to the 'interpretation' of Marx's theory and in particular to *Capital*. The particularly sensitive point: Volume One Part I, above all the 'labour theory of value', the theory of 'surplus-value' and the theory of the 'law of value'.

The above works can be obtained on demand in most specialist bookshops.

24. No English translation.
25. These works can be found in the English-language edition of Lenin's *Collected Works* (International Publishers) and also usually as separate pamphlets published by International Publishers or Progress publishers.

Lenin before Hegel

In a lecture now a year old, published in a small volume by Maspero under the title *Lenin and Philosophy*, I have attempted to prove that Lenin should be regarded as having made a crucial contribution to dialectical materialism, in that he made a real *discovery* with respect to Marx and Engels, and that this discovery can be summarized as follows: Marx's scientific theory did not lead to a new philosophy (called dialectical materialism), but to a new *practice* of philosophy, to be precise to the practice of philosophy based on a proletarian class position in philosophy.

This discovery, which I regard as essential, can be formulated in the following theses:

1. Philosophy is not a science, and it has no object, in the sense in which a science has an object.

2. Philosophy is a *practice* of political *intervention* carried out in a theoretical form.

3. It intervenes essentially in two privileged domains, the political domain of the effects of the class struggle and the theoretical domain of the effects of scientific practice.

4. In its essence, it is itself produced in the theoretical domain by the conjunction of the effects of the class struggle and the effects of scientific practice.

5. It therefore intervenes politically, in a theoretical

form, in the two domains, that of political practice and that of scientific practice: these two domains of intervention being *its* domains, insofar as it is itself produced by the combination of effects from these two practices.

6. All philosophy expresses a class position, a 'partisanship' in the great debate which dominates the whole history of philosophy, the debate between idealism and materialism.

7. The Marxist-Leninist revolution in philosophy consists of a rejection of the idealist conception of philosophy (philosophy as an 'interpretation of the world') which denies that philosophy expresses a class position, although it always does so itself, and the adoption of the proletarian class position in philosophy, which is materialist, i.e. the inauguration of a new materialist and revolutionary practice of philosophy which induces effects of class division in theory.

All these theses can be found in *Materialism and Empiriocriticism*, either explicitly or implicitly. All I have done is to begin to make them more explicit. *Materialism and Empiriocriticism* dates *from 1908*. At that time Lenin had not read, or not really read, Hegel. Lenin only read Hegel in 1914 and 1915. We should note that immediately before he read Hegel – the Little Logic (the *Encyclopedia*), then the Great Logic and the Philosophy of History – Lenin read Feuerbach (1914).

Hence Lenin read Feuerbach and Hegel in 1914–15, during the first two years of the inter-imperialist War, nine years after the crushing of the Revolution of October 1905, at the most critical moment in the History of the Workers' Movement, the moment of the treachery of the Social-Democratic Parties of the Second International, whose practice of a Holy Alliance inaugurated the great *split* which was to culminate in the gigantic work of Lenin and the Bolsheviks in the 1917 Revolution and in the foundation of the Third International.

Today, in April 1969, as we live through a second *de facto* split in the International Communist Movement, as the Chinese Communist Party holds its Ninth Congress and as preparations are being made for the International Conference of Communist Parties in Moscow, it is not at all irrelevant to reflect on Lenin in 1914–1915, reading Hegel's *Logic*. It is not scholasticism but philosophy, and since philosophy is politics in theory, *it is therefore politics*. We have an immense advantage over Lenin in that we are not living in a world war, and can see slightly more clearly into the future of the International Communist Movement, despite its present split, and perhaps even because of its present split, despite the meagreness of our information about it. For one can always reflect.

The paradox of Lenin's attitude before Hegel can be grasped by contrasting two facts:

1. *First fact*

In 1894, in *What the 'Friends of the People' Are*, Lenin, who had clearly not read Hegel, but only what Marx says about Hegel in the *Afterword* to the second German edition of *Capital*, and what Engels says about Hegel in *Anti-Dühring* and *Feuerbach and the End of Classical German Philosophy*, devotes a dozen pages to the difference between Marx's materialist dialectic and Hegel's dialectic! These twelve pages are a categorical declaration of anti-Hegelianism. The conclusion of these twelve pages (in a note) is, and I quote, '*the absurdity of accusing Marxism of Hegelian Dialectics*' (Lenin, *Collected Works*, Vol. 1, p. 174n.). Lenin quotes Marx's declaration that his '*method is the "direct opposite" of Hegel's method*' (p. 167). Asfor Marx's Hegelian formulations, the very ones which occur in *Capital*, in particular in Volume One Part I, which

Marx himself signalled as the result of his having 'coquetted (*kokettieren*) with the modes of expression peculiar to Hegel', Lenin settles accounts with them by saying that they are '*Marx's manner of expression*' and relate to '*the origin of the doctrine*', adding with much common sense that '*the theory should not be blamed for its origin*' (p. 164). Lenin goes on to say that the Hegelian formulations of the dialectic, the '*empty dialectical scheme*' of the triads, is a '*lid*' or a '*skin*' and that not only can one remove this lid or skin without changing anything in the bowl uncovered or the fruit peeled, but indeed they *must* be uncovered or peeled in order to see what is in them.

May I remind the reader that in 1894 Lenin had not read Hegel, but he had read Marx's *Capital* very closely, and understood it better than anyone else ever had – he was twenty-four – so much so that the best introduction to Marx's *Capital* is to be found in Lenin. Which would seem to prove that the best way to understand Hegel and the relation between Marx and Hegel is above all to have read and understood *Capital*.

2. *Second Fact*

In 1915, in his notes on the *Great Logic*, Lenin wrote a statement which everyone knows by heart, and which I quote: '*Aphorism: it is impossible completely to understand Marx's* Capital, *and especially its first chapter, without having thoroughly studied and understood the whole of Hegel's* Logic. *Consequently, half a century later none of the Marxists understood Marx!!*' (*Collected Works*, Vol. 38, p. 180 – Lenin's exclamation marks).

For any superficial reader, this statement obviously contradicts the statements of 1894, since instead of radical anti-Hegelian declarations, here we seem to have a radical pro-Hegelian declaration. Indeed, it goes so far that, if it were applied to Lenin himself, as the author of remarkable texts on *Capital* written between 1893 and 1905, he would appear as not having '*understood Marx*', since before 1914–1915, Lenin had not 'thoroughly studied and understood the whole of Hegel's *Logic*'!

I shall leave the conventional commentators to extricate themselves from this little 'contradiction', but I doubt whether they will make much progress with it, however much they declare, as good commentators on other texts of Lenin's, that 'contradiction' is the universal motor of all progress, including the progress of understanding. . . .

For myself, I state that I subscribe word for word to this second declaration of Lenin's just as I do to the first. I shall explain this directly. Lenin was quite right to say that to 'understand *Capital*', and especially, as he has the genius to point out, *its first chapter*, i.e. the extraordinary Volume One Part I, extraordinary because it is still Hegelian, not only in its terminology, but also in its order of exposition, it is essential to know Hegel's *Logic* through and through – and for good reason.

I can reduce the paradox of this second fact, of this second declaration of Lenin's straightaway by pointing out that it is preceded (a page earlier in the Notebooks) by another very interesting formula only a few lines before. Lenin declares, in fact, that '*Hegel's analysis of syllogisms . . . recalls Marx's imitation of Hegel in Ch. 1*'. This is a re-phrasing of Marx's own diagnosis: his 'coquetting' with Hegel. If the cap fits, wear it. This is not me speaking, but Lenin, following Marx. In fact, one cannot understand Volume One Part I at all without completely removing its Hegelian 'lid', without reading as a materialist, as Lenin reads Hegel, the said Volume One Part I, without, if you will forgive the presumption, *re-writing* it.

This brings us directly to my central thesis on Lenin's reading of Hegel: i.e. that *in his notes on Hegel, Lenin*

*maintains precisely the position he had adopted previously in
'What the "Friends of the People" Are' and 'Materialism
and Empirio-criticism'*, i.e. at a moment when he had not
read Hegel, which leads us to a 'shocking' but correct
conclusion: basically, Lenin did not need to read Hegel in
order to understand him, because he had already understood Hegel, having closely read and understood Marx.
Bearing this in mind, I shall hazard a peremptory aphorism
of my own: *'A century and a half later no one has understood
Hegel because it is impossible to understand Hegel without
having thoroughly studied and understood "Capital" !'* Provocation for provocation; I hope I shall be forgiven this one,
at least in the Marxist camp.

As for the Hegelians, they can carry on with their philosophical rumination in Hegel, Ruminator of all Ruminations,
i.e. the Interpreter of all the Interpretations in the history
of philosophy. At any rate, as good Hegelians, they know
that History is over and that therefore they can only go
round and round within the theory of the End of History,
i.e. in Hegel.

After all, it is not just roundabouts that go round and
round, the wheel of history can go round and round, too.
The wheel of philosophical history at least, which always
goes round and round, and when it is Hegelian, its advantage, like the advantage Pascal attributed to man over the
reed, is that *it 'knows it'*.

What, when, was so interesting to Lenin in Hegel's *Great
Logic*?

In order to answer this question, we must first learn to
read Lenin's notes on his reading of Hegel. This is a truism,
but one from which, of course, hardly anyone draws the
necessary, but elementary, conclusions. We have to believe
that none of the commentators of the *Notebooks* on Hegel

have ever themselves kept a book of notes on their own individual reading.

For when one takes notes, there are notes whose function it is to summarize what one has just read, and there are notes whose function it is to assess what one has just read. There are also notes that one takes, and notes that one does not take. For example, those who are prepared to compare the text of Hegel's *Great Logic* with the text of Lenin's notes cannot fail to observe that Lenin almost completely ignores the Book on *Being*, leaving hardly any comment on it other than summarizing notes. This is surely strange, i.e. symptomatic. These same readers cannot fail to remark that the notes become abundant (and not just the summarizing notes, but also the critical notes, usually approving but occasionally disapproving) when Lenin comes to the Book on *Essence*, which clearly interests him considerably; and that Lenin's notes become very abundant for the Book devoted to *Subjective Logic* and very laudatory on the *Absolute Idea*, the Chapter on which Lenin, amazing though it may seem, regards as practically *materialist*.

I cannot go into all the details, although they are essential, but I attach the greatest importance to a critical, i.e. a materialist, reading of Lenin's Notes on his reading of Hegel, in order, first, to say how Lenin reads Hegel, then, to say what primarily interests him in Hegel, and finally, to attempt to say why.

I. HOW LENIN READ HEGEL.
He read Hegel, and the phrase constantly recurs, as a 'materialist'. What does this phrase mean?

First, it means that Lenin read Hegel by 'inverting' him. What does this 'inversion' mean? Simply the 'inversion' of idealism into materialism. But beware! In practice this means *not* that Lenin put matter in place of the Idea and *vice versa*, for that would merely produce a new materialist metaphysics (i.e. a materialist variant of classical philosophy, say, at best a mechanistic materialism), but that for his reading of Hegel, Lenin adopted a proletarian *class viewpoint* (a dialectical-materialist viewpoint), which is something quite different.

In other words, Lenin did not read Hegel in order to set Hegel's absolute-idealist system back on to its feet in the form of a materialist system. For his reading of Hegel he adopted a new philosophical *practice*, a practice which followed from the proletarian class viewpoint, i.e. from the dialectical-materialist viewpoint. What interested Lenin in Hegel was above all the effects of this dialectical-materialist reading of Hegel, i.e. the effects produced with respect to a reading of passages from Hegel which deal primarily with what is called the 'theory of knowledge' and the dialectic.

If Lenin did not read Hegel according to the method of 'inversion', how did he read him? Precisely according to the method he described as early as 1894 in *What the 'Friends of the People' Are* with respect to the reading of *Capital* Volume One Part I: by the method of *'laying bare'*. What is valid for the reading of passages from Marx contaminated by Hegelian terminology and the Hegelian order of exposition in *Capital* is obviously valid *a fortiori*, a hundred times *a fortiori*, for Hegel himself. Hence the radical *laying bare*. A central passage in the *Notebooks* says this in so many words:

Movement and 'self-movement' (this NB! arbitrary (independent), spontaneous, internally-necessary movement), 'change', 'movement and vitality', 'the principle of all self-movement,' 'impulse' (*Trieb*) to 'movement' and to 'activity' – the opposite to 'dead Being' – who would believe that this is the core of 'Hegelianism', of abstract and *abstrusen* (ponderous, absurd?) Hegelianism?? This core had to be *discovered, understood, hinüberretten, laid bare, refined*, which is precisely what Marx and Engels did (op. cit., Vol. 38, p. 141).

What are we to understand by this metaphor of 'laying bare', 'refining' or 'extraction' (a term used elsewhere), if not the image that there is in Hegel something like a 'rational' kernel which must be rid of its skin, or better no doubt, of its superimposed skins, in short of a certain crust which is more or less thick (think of a fruit, an onion, or even an artichoke). Hence the extraction needs to be laboriously laid bare. Sometimes, as in the Chapter on the Absolute Idea, the materialist kernel reaches almost to the surface, a mere laying bare is enough. Sometimes, the skin is thick, it is tangled with the kernel itself, and the kernel needs to be disentangled. In either case, a labour involving more or less transformation is necessary. Sometimes there is only the skin: nothing at all to retain, *everything has to be discarded*, there is no rational kernel. Thus in the Book of the *Great Logic* on Being, and in all the passages containing, directly or indirectly, what Lenin calls 'mysticism' (e.g. where logic is alienated into Nature), Lenin writes furiously: 'stupidity! foolishness! incredible!', and he rejects outright 'nonsense about the absolute. I am in general trying to read Hegel materialistically: Hegel is materialism which has been stood on its head (according to Engels) – that is to say, I cast aside for the most part God, the Absolute, the Pure Idea, etc.' (p. 104).

Thus a rather special method. The inversion is simply an affirmation of the partisan position of the proletariat in philosophy: the inversion of idealism into materialism. The real operation, the real *work of materialist reading* consists of a quite different operation:

1. the rejection of a mass of propositions and theses with which nothing can be done, from which absolutely nothing can be obtained, skins without kernels;

2. the retention of certain well-chosen fruits and vege-
tables, and their careful peeling or the disentanglement of
their kernels from their thick skins, tangled with the kernel,
by real transforming work. 'One must first of all *extract* the
materialist dialectics from it (the Hegelian galimatias).
Nine-tenths of it, however, is chaff, rubbish' (p. 154).

What a waste! This has nothing to do with the miraculous
'inversion'.

II. WHAT IS IT THAT INTERESTS LENIN?

What is it that Lenin retains from Hegel and re-works?

Here I could go on for ever. I shall group my points
under the two chapter headings which are the most important in my eyes, and, I believe, in the eyes of every careful
reader of the *Notebooks*. The first deals with Hegel's
criticism of Kant, the second with the Chapter on the
Absolute Idea.

A. Hegel's Criticism of Kant

This never fails; whenever Lenin finds a criticism of
Kant in Hegel's text, he approves. And especially when
Hegel criticizes the Kantian notion of the thing-in-itself
as unknowable. Then Lenin's approval is categorical and
even lyrical:

Essentially, Hegel is completely right as opposed to Kant. Thought
proceeding from the concrete to the abstract . . . does not get away
from the truth but comes closer to it. The abstraction of matter, of a
law of nature, the abstraction of value, etc., in short *all* scientific
(correct, serious, not absurd) abstractions reflect nature more deeply,
truly and *completely*. From living perception to abstract thought, and
from this to practice – such is the dialectical path of the cognition of
truth, of the cognition of objective reality. Kant disparages knowledge
in order to make way for faith: Hegel exalts knowledge, asserting that
knowledge is knowledge of God. The materialist exalts the knowledge
of matter, of nature, consigning God, and the philosophical rabble
that defends God, to the rubbish heap (op. cit., Vol. 38, p. 171).

Here Lenin is merely repeating Engels:

> In addition there is yet a set of different philosophers – those who question the possibility of any cognition, or at least of an exhaustive cognition of the world. To them, among the more modern ones, belong Hume and Kant, and they have played a very important role in philosophical development. What is decisive in the refutation of this view has already been said by Hegel, *in so far as this was possible from an idealist standpoint* ('Feuerbach and the End of Classical German Philosophy', Marx-Engels: *Selected Works*, London, 1968, p. 605).

How are we to interpret this attitude? We should note carefully that when Lenin approves of the fact that Hegel criticizes Kant from a Hegelian viewpoint, he certainly does not approve of the Hegelian viewpoint 100 per cent, but he does approve 100 per cent of the fact that Kant is criticized, and, let us say, approves of a large part of the arguments behind Hegel's criticism of Kant. This is really an obvious point: it is possible for two people to be in agreement against a third party for different reasons, more or less different reasons.

For Lenin, as for Hegel, Kant means *subjectivism*.[1] In a quasi-Hegelian phrase, Lenin says that the transcendental is subjectivism and psychology. And naturally we are not surprised to find that Lenin occasionally compares Kant with Mach. Hence Lenin is in agreement with Hegel in criticizing Kant from the point of view of *objectivism* . . . but what objectivism? We shall see.

In any case, he delights in Hegel's criticism of the thing-in-itself. An empty notion, he says, in agreement with the Hegelian formulation, it is a myth to claim to be able to think the unknowable, the thing-in-itself is the identity of the essence in the phenomenon.

1. 'Hegel charges Kant with subjectivism. This NB. Hegel is for the "objective rationality" . . . of Semblance, " of that which is immediately given".' (op. cit., Vol. 38, p. 134).

In Kant, *Ding an sich* is an empty abstraction, but Hegel demands abstraction which corresponds to *der Sache* (op. cit., p. 92).

In this dual theme: the categorical rejection of the thing-in-itself – and its counterpart: the existence of the essence in the phenomenon, which Lenin reads as the identity of the essence and the thing-in-itself (the essence identical with its phenomenon), Lenin is in agreement with Hegel, though the latter would not say that the 'reality' of the thing-in-itself is the essence. A shade of meaning perhaps, but an important one.

Why is it important? Because Hegel's criticism of Kant is a criticism of subjective idealism in the name of absolute idealism, which means that Hegel does not stop at a Theory of the Essence, but criticizes Kant in the name of a Theory of the Idea, *whereas Lenin stops at what Hegel would call a Theory of the Essence.*

Here we see 'in the name of what' Lenin criticizes Kant's subjectivism: in the name of *objectivism*, I have said. This term is too easily a pendant of the term subjectivism for it not to be immediately suspect. Let us say rather that Lenin criticizes Kant's subjectivism in the name of a materialist thesis which is a thesis conjointly of (material) existence and of (scientific) objectivity. In other words, Lenin criticizes Kant from the viewpoint of *philosophical materialism* and *scientific objectivity*, thought together in the thesis of materialism. This is precisely the position of *Materialism and Empirio-criticism.*

But it enables us to reveal a number of important consequences nonetheless. Let us run through them.

The critique of Kant's transcendental subjectivism contained in the selective reading in which Lenin 'lays bare' Hegel entails:

1. the elimination of the thing-in-itself and its reconversion into the dialectical action of the identity of essence and phenomenon;

2. the elimination of the category of the Subject (whether transcendental or otherwise);

3. with this double elimination and the reconversion of the thing-in-itself into the dialectical action of the essence in its phenomenon, Lenin produces an effect often underlined in *Materialism and Empirio-criticism*: the *liberation of scientific practice*, finally freed from every dogma that would make it an ossified thing, thus restoring to it its rightful living existence – this life of science merely reflecting the life of reality itself.[2]

This is the categorical limit dividing Lenin from Hegel in their criticisms of Kant. For Lenin, Hegel criticizes Kant from the viewpoint of the Absolute Idea, i.e. provisionally, of 'God' – whereas Lenin uses Hegel's criticism of Kant to criticize Kant *from the viewpoint of science*, of scientific objectivity and its correlate, the material existence of its object.

This is the practice of laying-bare and peeling, of refining, as we can see it at a point *where it is possible*: Lenin takes what interests him from his point of view from the discourse which Hegel is pursuing from a quite different point of view. What determines the principle of the choice is the difference in viewpoints: the primacy of science and its material object, for Lenin; whereas, as we know, for Hegel, science, meaning the science of the scientists (which remains in the Intellect), has no primacy: since in Hegel

---

2. '*Sehr gut*!! If we ask what Things-in-themselves are, so *ist in die Frage gedankenloser Weise die Unmöglichkeit der Beantwortung gelegt* [the question, in thoughtlessness, is so put as to render an answer impossible] . . . This is very profound: . . . the Thing-in-itself is altogether an empty, lifeless abstraction. In life, in movement, each thing and everything is *usually* both "in itself" and "for others" in relation to an Other, being transformed from one state to the other' (p. 109). 'In Kant [we have] "the empty abstraction" of the Thing-in-itself instead of living *Gang, Bewegung*, deeper and deeper, of our knowledge about things' (op. cit., p. 91).

science is subject to the primacy of Religion and Philosophy, which is the truth of Religion.

B. The Chapter on the Absolute Idea

We move from paradox to paradox. I have just said that what interests Lenin in Hegel is the criticism of Kant, but from the point of view of scientific objectivity – and not from the point of view of its truth, which, to be brief, is represented in Hegel by the Absolute Idea. And yet, Lenin is passionately interested in the Chapter on the Absolute Idea, which he sees as almost materialist:

> It is noteworthy that the whole chapter on the 'Absolute Idea' scarcely says a word about God (hardly ever has a 'divine' 'notion' slipped out accidentally) and apart from that – *this NB* – it contains almost nothing that is specifically idealism, but has for its main subject the dialectical method. The sum-total, the last word and essence of Hegel's logic is *the dialectical method* – this is extremely noteworthy. And one thing more: in this *most idealistic* of Hegel's works there is the least idealism and the *most materialism*. 'Contradictory', but a fact! (op. cit., p. 234).

How are we to explain this paradox?

Ultimately in a fairly simple way. But before doing so, I must go back a little.

Last year, in a paper I read at Jean Hyppolite's seminar, I showed what Marx owed to Hegel in theory. After critically examining the dialectic of what may be called the conceptual experiment carried out by Marx in the *1884 Manuscripts*, where Feuerbach's theory of the alienation of the Human Essence underwent a Hegelian injection, precisely the injection of the *process of historical alienation* – I was able to show that this combination was untenable and explosive, and in fact it was abandoned by Marx on the one hand (the Manuscripts were not published and their theses were progressively abandoned later), while on the other it produced an *explosion*.

The untenable thesis upheld by Marx in the *1844 Manuscripts* was that History is the History of the process of alienation of a Subject, the Generic Essence of Man alienated in 'alienated labour'.

But it was precisely this thesis that *exploded*. The result of this explosion was the evaporation of the notions of subject, human essence, and alienation, which disappear, completely atomized, and the liberation of the concept of a *process* (*procès* or *processus*) *without a subject*, which is the basis of all the analyses in *Capital*.

Marx himself provides evidence of this in a note to the French edition of *Capital* (this is interesting, for Marx must have added this note three or four years after the appearance of the German edition, i.e. after an interval which had allowed him to grasp the importance of this category and to express it to himself). This is what Marx wrote:

> The word *'procès'* (process) which expresses *a development considered in the totality of its real conditions* has long been part of scientific language throughout Europe. In France it was first introduced slightly shamefacedly in its Latin form – *processus*. Then, stripped of this pedantic disguise, it slipped into books on chemistry, physics, physiology, etc., and into a few works of metaphysics. In the end it will obtain a certificate of complete naturalization. Let us note in passing that in ordinary speech the Germans, like the French use the word *Prozess* (*procès*, process) in the legal sense [i.e. trial] (*Le Capital*, Éditions Sociales, t.I, p. 181n.).

Now, for anyone who 'knows' how to read Hegel's *Logic* as a materialist, a process without a subject is precisely what can be found in the Chapter on the Absolute Idea. Jean Hyppolite decisively proved that Hegel's conception of history had absolutely nothing to do with any anthropology. The proof: History is the Spirit, it is the last moment of the alienation of a process which 'begins' with Logic, continues with Nature and ends with the Spirit, the Spirit, i.e. what can be presented in the form of 'History'. For Hegel, quite to the contrary of the erroneous view of Kojève and the young Lukács, and of others since them, who are almost ashamed of the Dialectics of Nature, the dialectic is by no means peculiar to History, which means that History does not contain anywhere in itself, in any subject, its own origin. The Marxist tradition was quite correct to return to the thesis of the Dialectics of Nature, which has the polemical meaning[3] that history is a *process without a subject*, that the dialectic at work in history is not the work of any Subject whatsoever, whether Absolute (God) or merely human, but that the origin of history is always already thrust back before history, and therefore that there is neither a philosophical origin nor a philosophical subject to History. Now what matters to us here is that Nature itself is not, in Hegel's eyes, its own origin; it is itself the result of a process of alienation which does not begin with it: i.e. of a process whose origin is elsewhere – in Logic.

This is where the question becomes really fascinating. For it is clear that Lenin swept aside in one sentence the absurd idea that Nature was a product of the alienation of Logic, and yet he says that the Chapter on the Absolute Idea is quasi-materialist. Surprising.

What, in fact, is the status of Logic in Hegel? It is double: on the one hand, Logic is the origin itself, that which it is impossible to go back beyond, and that with which the ulterior process of alienation begins. Hence this process of alienation does seem to have a Subject: Logic. But when

3. Among others.

we examine closely the 'nature' of this Subject which is supposed to be Absolute, precisely in the Chapter on the Absolute Idea, we find that it is *the origin negated as an origin*. This can be seen at two points in particular.

Firstly, at the beginning of the *Logic*, which negates what it begins with from the very beginning, by immediately negating being in nothingness, which can only mean one thing: the origin must simultaneously be affirmed and negated, hence the subject must be negated *from the moment* that it is posited.

Secondly, in Hegel's famous thesis that the Absolute Idea is simply the absolute method, the method which, as it is nothing but the very movement of the process, is merely the idea of the process as the only Absolute.

Lenin applies his materialist reading to this double thesis of Hegel's. And that is why he is so fascinated by the Absolute Idea. He thus lays bare and refines this notion, too, retaining the Absolute, but *rejecting the Idea*, which amounts to saying that Lenin takes from Hegel the following proposition: there is only one thing in the world which is absolute, and that is the method or the concept of the process, itself absolute. And as Hegel himself suggested by the beginning of Logic, being = nothingness, and by the very place of Logic, origin negated as origin, Subject negated as Subject, Lenin finds in it a confirmation of the fact that it is absolutely essential (as he had learnt simply from a thorough-going reading of *Capital*) *to suppress every origin and every subject, and to say*: what is absolute is *the process without a subject*, both in reality and in scientific knowledge.

As this proposition breaks through, i.e. constantly touches the surface, or rather the *skin*, all that is needed is to *lay it bare* to obtain the Marxist-Leninist concept of the *materialist dialectic*, of the absoluteness of movement, of the absolute process of the reality of the method: to be precise, the

concept of the fundamental scientific validity of the concept
of a *process without a subject*, as it is to be found in *Capital*,
and elsewhere, too, in Freud, for example.

The materialist thesis of the material existence and of the
objectivity of scientific knowledge thus finds a confirmation
which is both radical and disconcerting here in the Chapter
on the Absolute Idea. Completely disconcerting for a
reader of Hegel who has not read Marx, but completely
natural for a reader of Hegel who has read Marx. I would
even say, completely natural for anyone who, without
having read Hegel, could speak of him in complete ignorance, i.e. in complete knowledge of the situation, in the
strongest sense – like the twenty-four-year-old who, in
1894, wrote the twelve pages on Hegel that I have discussed.

With these comments as starting-point, I ask you in your
turn to try to re-read Lenin reading Hegel, and to tell me
if the shocking proposition I put forward a moment ago is
not the very truth:

*A century and a half later no one has understood Hegel
because it is impossible to understand Hegel without having
thoroughly studied and understood 'Capital'.*

Thanks to Lenin, we can begin, not to read or to interpret,
but to understand the Hegelian philosophical world, while
transforming it, of course.

Allow me to recall that this divination of Hegel by Lenin,
and then his reading of Hegel, were only possible from a
proletarian class viewpoint, and with the new practice of
philosophy that follows from it. Perhaps we can learn a
lesson from this for the present and the future. For all in
all the situation in 1969 is less serious for the International
Marxist Workers' Movement than it was in 1915 – which
does not mean that the task is not immense – it is only less
difficult, despite appearances. On one condition, which Marx
demanded of his reader, on the threshold of *Capital*: that

he has the courage to *'think for himself'* and about what is in preparation, even at moderate or long distance, what is in preparation among the masses, for it is they and not the philosophers who make history.

April 1969

Ideology and Ideological State Apparatuses (Notes towards an Investigation)

ON THE REPRODUCTION OF THE CONDITIONS OF PRODUCTION[1]

I must now expose more fully something which was briefly glimpsed in my analysis when I spoke of the necessity to renew the means of production if production is to be possible. That was a passing hint. Now I shall consider it for itself.

As Marx said, every child knows that a social formation which did not reproduce the conditions of production at the same time as it produced would not last a year.[2] The ultimate condition of production is therefore the reproduction of the conditions of production. This may be 'simple' (reproducing exactly the previous conditions of production) or 'on an extended scale' (expanding them). Let us ignore this last distinction for the moment.

What, then, is *the reproduction of the conditions of production?*

Here we are entering a domain which is both very fam-

1. This text is made up of two extracts from an ongoing study. The sub-title 'Notes towards an Investigation' is the author's own. The ideas expounded should not be regarded as more than the introduction to a discussion.
2. Marx to Kugelmann, 11 July 1868, *Selected Correspondence*, Moscow, 1955, p. 209.

iliar (since *Capital* Volume Two) and uniquely ignored. The tenacious obviousnesses (ideological obviousnesses of an empiricist type) of the point of view of production alone, or even of that of mere productive practice (itself abstract in relation to the process of production) are so integrated into our everyday 'consciousness' that it is extremely hard, not to say almost impossible, to raise oneself to the *point of view of reproduction*. Nevertheless, everything outside this point of view remains abstract (worse than one-sided: distorted) – even at the level of production, and, *a fortiori*, at that of mere practice.

Let us try and examine the matter methodically.

To simplify my exposition, and assuming that every social formation arises from a dominant mode of production, I can say that the process of production sets to work the existing productive forces in and under definite relations of production.

It follows that, in order to exist, every social formation must reproduce the conditions of its production at the same time as it produces, and in order to be able to produce. It must therefore reproduce:

1. the productive forces,
2. the existing relations of production.

Reproduction of the Means of Production

Everyone (including the bourgeois economists whose work is national accounting, or the modern 'macro-economic' 'theoreticians') now recognizes, because Marx compellingly proved it in *Capital* Volume Two, that no production is possible which does not allow for the reproduction of the material conditions of production: the reproduction of the means of production.

The average economist, who is no different in this than

the average capitalist, knows that each year it is essential to foresee what is needed to replace what has been used up or worn out in production: raw material, fixed installations (buildings), instruments of production (machines), etc. I say the average economist = the average capitalist, for they both express the point of view of the firm, regarding it as sufficient simply to give a commentary on the terms of the firm's financial accounting practice.

But thanks to the genius of Quesnay who first posed this 'glaring' problem, and to the genius of Marx who resolved it, we know that the reproduction of the material conditions of production cannot be thought at the level of the firm, because it does not exist at that level in its real conditions. What happens at the level of the firm is an effect, which only gives an idea of the necessity of reproduction, but absolutely fails to allow its conditions and mechanisms to be thought.

A moment's reflection is enough to be convinced of this: Mr X, a capitalist who produces woollen yarn in his spinning-mill, has to 'reproduce' his raw material, his machines, etc. But *he* does not produce them for his own production – other capitalists do: an Australian sheep-farmer, Mr Y, a heavy engineer producing machine-tools, Mr Z, etc., etc. And Mr Y and Mr Z, in order to produce those products which are the condition of the reproduction of Mr X's conditions of production, also have to reproduce the conditions of their own production, and so on to infinity – the whole in proportions such that, on the national and even the world market, the demand for means of production (for reproduction) can be satisfied by the supply.

In order to think this mechanism, which leads to a kind of 'endless chain', it is necessary to follow Marx's 'global' procedure, and to study in particular the relations of the circulation of capital between Department I (production of means of production) and Department II (production of means of consumption), and the realization of surplus-value, in *Capital*, Volumes Two and Three.

We shall not go into the analysis of this question. It is enough to have mentioned the existence of the necessity of the reproduction of the material conditions of production.

Reproduction of Labour-Power

However, the reader will not have failed to note one thing. We have discussed the reproduction of the means of production – but not the reproduction of the productive forces. We have therefore ignored the reproduction of what distinguishes the productive forces from the means of production, i.e. the reproduction of labour power.

From the observation of what takes place in the firm, in particular from the examination of the financial accounting practice which predicts amortization and investment, we have been able to obtain an approximate idea of the existence of the material process of reproduction, but we are now entering a domain in which the observation of what happens in the firm is, if not totally blind, at least almost entirely so, and for good reason: the reproduction of labour power takes place essentially outside the firm.

How is the reproduction of labour power ensured?

It is ensured by giving labour power the material means with which to reproduce itself: by wages. Wages feature in the accounting of each enterprise, but as 'wage capital',[3] not at all as a condition of the material reproduction of labour power.

However, that is in fact how it 'works', since wages represents only that part of the value produced by the expendi-

3. Marx gave it its scientific concept: *variable capital*.

ture of labour power which is indispensable for its reproduction: sc. indispensable to the reconstitution of the
labour power of the wage-earner (the wherewithal to pay
for housing, food and clothing, in short to enable the wage-
earner to present himself again at the factory gate the next
day – and every further day God grants him); and we should
add: indispensable for raising and educating the children
in whom the proletarian reproduces himself (in n models
where n = 0, 1, 2, etc. . . .) as labour power.

Remember that this quantity of value (wages) necessary
for the reproduction of labour power is determined not by
the needs of a 'biological' Guaranteed Minimum Wage
(*Salaire Minimum Interprofessionnel Garanti*) alone, but by
the needs of a historical minimum (Marx noted that
English workers need beer while French proletarians need
wine) – i.e. a historically variable minimum.

I should also like to point out that this minimum is doubly
historical in that it is not defined by the historical needs of
the working class 'recognized' by the capitalist class, but
by the historical needs imposed by the proletarian class
struggle (a double class struggle: against the lengthening
of the working day and against the reduction of wages).

However, it is not enough to ensure for labour power the
material conditions of its reproduction if it is to be reproduced as labour power. I have said that the available labour
power must be 'competent', i.e. suitable to be set to work
in the complex system of the process of production. The
development of the productive forces and the type of unity
historically constitutive of the productive forces at a given
moment produce the result that the labour power has to be
(diversely) skilled and therefore reproduced as such.
Diversely: according to the requirements of the socio-
technical division of labour, its different 'jobs' and 'posts'.

How is this reproduction of the (diversified) skills of

labour power provided for in a capitalist regime? Here, unlike social formations characterized by slavery or serfdom, this reproduction of the skills of labour power tends (this is a tendential law) decreasingly to be provided for 'on the spot' (apprenticeship within production itself), but is achieved more and more outside production: by the capitalist education system, and by other instances and institutions.

What do children learn at school? They go varying distances in their studies, but at any rate they learn to read, to write and to add – i.e. a number of techniques, and a number of other things as well, including elements (which may be rudimentary or on the contrary thoroughgoing) of 'scientific' or 'literary culture', which are directly useful in the different jobs in production (one instruction for manual workers, another for technicians, a third for engineers, a final one for higher management, etc.). Thus they learn 'know-how'.

But besides these techniques and knowledges, and in learning them, children at school also learn the 'rules' of good behaviour, i.e. the attitude that should be observed by every agent in the division of labour, according to the job he is 'destined' for: rules of morality, civic and professional conscience, which actually means rules of respect for the socio-technical division of labour and ultimately the rules of the order established by class domination. They also learn to 'speak proper French', to 'handle' the workers correctly, i.e. actually (for the future capitalists and their servants) to 'order them about' properly, i.e. (ideally) to 'speak to them' in the right way, etc.

To put this more scientifically, I shall say that the reproduction of labour power requires not only a reproduction of its skills, but also, at the same time, a reproduction of its submission to the rules of the established order, i.e. a reproduction of submission to the ruling ideology for the workers, and a reproduction of the ability to manipulate the ruling ideology correctly for the agents of exploitation and repression, so that they, too, will provide for the domination of the ruling class 'in words'.

In other words, the school (but also other State institutions like the Church, or other apparatuses like the Army) teaches 'know-how', but in forms which ensure *subjection to the ruling ideology* or the mastery of its 'practice'. All the agents of production, exploitation and repression, not to speak of the 'professionals of ideology' (Marx), must in one way or another be 'steeped' in this ideology in order to perform their tasks 'conscientiously' – the tasks of the exploited (the proletarians), of the exploiters (the capitalists), of the exploiters' auxiliaries (the managers), or of the high priests of the ruling ideology (its 'functionaries'), etc.

The reproduction of labour power thus reveals as its *sine qua non* not only the reproduction of its 'skills' but also the reproduction of its subjection to the ruling ideology or of the 'practice' of that ideology, with the proviso that it is not enough to say 'not only but also', for it is clear that *it is in the forms and under the forms of ideological subjection that provision is made for the reproduction of the skills of labour power*.

But this is to recognize the effective presence of a new reality: *ideology*.

Here I shall make two comments.

The first is to round off my analysis of reproduction.

I have just given a rapid survey of the forms of the reproduction of the productive forces, i.e. of the means of production on the one hand, and of labour power on the other.

But I have not yet approached the question of the *reproduction of the relations of production*. This is a *crucial question* for the Marxist theory of the mode of production.

To let it pass would be a theoretical omission – worse, a serious political error.

I shall therefore discuss it. But in order to obtain the means to discuss it, I shall have to make another long detour.

The second comment is that in order to make this detour, I am obliged to re-raise my old question: what is a society?

INFRASTRUCTURE AND SUPERSTRUCTURE

On a number of occasions[4] I have insisted on the revolutionary character of the Marxist conception of the 'social whole' insofar as it is distinct from the Hegelian 'totality'. I said (and this thesis only repeats famous propositions of historical materialism) that Marx conceived the structure of every society as constituted by 'levels' or 'instances' articulated by a specific determination: the *infrastructure*, or economic base (the 'unity' of the productive forces and the relations of production) and the *superstructure*, which itself contains two 'levels' or 'instances': the politico-legal (law and the State) and ideology (the different ideologies, religious, ethical, legal, political, etc.).

Besides its theoretico-didactic interest (it reveals the difference between Marx and Hegel), this representation has the following crucial theoretical advantage: it makes it possible to inscribe in the theoretical apparatus of its essential concepts what I have called their *respective indices of effectivity*. What does this mean?

It is easy to see that this representation of the structure of every society as an edifice containing a base (infrastruc-

4. In *For Marx* and *Reading Capital*, 1965 (English editions 1969 and 1970 respectively).

ture) on which are erected the two 'floors' of the superstructure, is a metaphor, to be quite precise, a spatial metaphor: the metaphor of a topography (*topique*).[5] Like every
metaphor, this metaphor suggests something, makes something visible. What? Precisely this: that the upper floors
could not 'stay up' (in the air) alone, if they did not rest
precisely on their base.

Thus the object of the metaphor of the edifice is to
represent above all the 'determination in the last instance'
by the economic base. The effect of this spatial metaphor
is to endow the base with an index of effectivity known by
the famous terms: the determination in the last instance
of what happens in the upper 'floors' (of the superstructure)
by what happens in the economic base.

Given this index of effectivity 'in the last instance', the
'floors' of the superstructure are clearly endowed with
different indices of effectivity. What kind of indices?

It is possible to say that the floors of the superstructure
are not determinant in the last instance, but that they are
determined by the effectivity of the base; that if they are
determinant in their own (as yet undefined) ways, this is
true only insofar as they are determined by the base.

Their index of effectivity (or determination), as determined by the determination in the last instance of the
base, is thought by the Marxist tradition in two ways: (1)
there is a 'relative autonomy' of the superstructure with
respect to the base; (2) there is a 'reciprocal action' of the
superstructure on the base.

We can therefore say that the great theoretical advantage
of the Marxist topography, i.e. of the spatial metaphor of

5. *Topography* from the Greek *topos*: place. A topography represents in a
definite space the respective *sites* occupied by several realities: thus the
economic is *at the bottom* (the base), the superstructure *above it*.

the edifice (base and superstructure) is simultaneously that it reveals that questions of determination (or of index of effectivity) are crucial; that it reveals that it is the base which in the last instance determines the whole edifice; and that, as a consequence, it obliges us to pose the theoretical problem of the types of 'derivatory' effectivity peculiar to the superstructure, i.e. it obliges us to think what the Marxist tradition calls conjointly the relative autonomy of the superstructure and the reciprocal action of the superstructure on the base.

The greatest disadvantage of this representation of the structure of every society by the spatial metaphor of an edifice, is obviously the fact that it is metaphorical: i.e. it remains *descriptive*.

It now seems to me that it is possible and desirable to represent things differently. NB, I do not mean by this that I want to reject the classical metaphor, for that metaphor itself requires that we go beyond it. And I am not going beyond it in order to reject it as outworn. I simply want to attempt to think what it gives us in the form of a description.

I believe that it is possible and necessary to think what characterizes the essential of the existence and nature of the superstructure *on the basis of reproduction*. Once one takes the point of view of reproduction, many of the questions whose existence was indicated by the spatial metaphor of the edifice, but to which it could not give a conceptual answer, are immediately illuminated.

My basic thesis is that it is not possible to pose these questions (and therefore to answer them) *except from the point of view of reproduction*.

I shall give a short analysis of Law, the State and Ideology *from this point of view*. And I shall reveal what happens both from the point of view of practice and production on the one hand, and from that of reproduction on the other.

THE STATE

The Marxist tradition is strict, here: in the *Communist Manifesto* and the *Eighteenth Brumaire* (and in all the later classical texts, above all in Marx's writings on the Paris Commune and Lenin's on *State and Revolution*), the State is explicitly conceived as a repressive apparatus. The State is a 'machine' of repression, which enables the ruling classes (in the nineteenth century the bourgeois class and the 'class' of big landowners) to ensure their domination over the working class, thus enabling the former to subject the latter to the process of surplus-value extortion (i.e. to capitalist exploitation).

The State is thus first of all what the Marxist classics have called *the State apparatus*. This term means: not only the specialized apparatus (in the narrow sense) whose existence and necessity I have recognized in relation to the requirements of legal practice, i.e. the police, the courts, the prisons; but also the army, which (the proletariat has paid for this experience with its blood) intervenes directly as a supplementary repressive force in the last instance, when the police and its specialized auxiliary corps are 'outrun by events'; and above this ensemble, the head of State, the government and the administration.

Presented in this form, the Marxist-Leninist 'theory' of the State has its finger on the essential point, and not for one moment can there be any question of rejecting the fact that this really is the essential point. The State apparatus, which defines the State as a force of repressive execution and intervention 'in the interests of the ruling classes' in the class struggle conducted by the bourgeoisie and its allies against the proletariat, is quite certainly the State, and quite certainly defines its basic 'function'.

From Descriptive Theory to Theory as such

Nevertheless, here too, as I pointed out with respect to the metaphor of the edifice (infrastructure and superstructure), this presentation of the nature of the State is still partly descriptive.

As I shall often have occasion to use this adjective (descriptive), a word of explanation is necessary in order to remove any ambiguity.

Whenever, in speaking of the metaphor of the edifice or of the Marxist 'theory' of the State, I have said that these are descriptive conceptions or representations of their objects, I had no ulterior critical motives. On the contrary, I have every grounds to think that great scientific discoveries cannot help but pass through the phase of what I shall call *descriptive 'theory'*. This is the first phase of every theory, at least in the domain which concerns us (that of the science of social formations). As such, one might – and in my opinion one must – envisage this phase as a transitional one, necessary to the development of the theory. That it is transitional is inscribed in my expression: 'descriptive theory', which reveals in its conjunction of terms the equivalent of a kind of 'contradiction'. In fact, the term theory 'clashes' to some extent with the adjective 'descriptive' which I have attached to it. This means quite precisely: (1) that the 'descriptive theory' really is, without a shadow of a doubt, the irreversible beginning of the theory; but (2) that the 'descriptive' form in which the theory is presented requires, precisely as an effect of this 'contradiction', a development of the theory which goes beyond the form of 'description'.

Let me make this idea clearer by returning to our present object: the State.

When I say that the Marxist 'theory' of the State available to us is still partly 'descriptive', that means first and foremost that this descriptive 'theory' is without the shadow of a doubt precisely the beginning of the Marxist theory of the State, and that this beginning gives us the essential point, i.e. the decisive principle of every later development of the theory.

Indeed, I shall call the descriptive theory of the State correct, since it is perfectly possible to make the vast majority of the facts in the domain with which it is concerned correspond to the definition it gives of its object. Thus, the definition of the State as a class State, existing in the repressive State apparatus, casts a brilliant light on all the facts observable in the various orders of repression whatever their domains: from the massacres of June 1848 and of the Paris Commune, of Bloody Sunday, May 1905 in Petrograd, of the Resistance, of Charonne, etc., to the mere (and relatively anodyne) interventions of a 'censorship' which has banned Diderot's *La Réligieuse* or a play by Gatti on Franco; it casts light on all the direct or indirect forms of exploitation and extermination of the masses of the people (imperialist wars); it casts light on that subtle everyday domination beneath which can be glimpsed, in the forms of political democracy, for example, what Lenin, following Marx, called the dictatorship of the bourgeoisie.

And yet the descriptive theory of the State represents a phase in the constitution of the theory which itself demands the 'supersession' of this phase. For it is clear that if the definition in question really does give us the means to identify and recognize the facts of oppression by relating them to the State, conceived as the repressive State apparatus, this 'interrelationship' gives rise to a very special kind of obviousness, about which I shall have something to say in a moment: 'Yes, that's how it is, that's really true!'[6]

6. See p. 158 below, *On Ideology*.

And the accumulation of facts within the definition of the State may multiply examples, but it does not really advance the definition of the State, i.e. the scientific theory of the State. Every descriptive theory thus runs the risk of 'blocking' the development of the theory, and yet that development is essential.

That is why I think that, in order to develop this descriptive theory into theory as such, i.e. in order to understand further the mechanisms of the State in its functioning, I think that it is indispensable to *add* something to the classical definition of the State as a State apparatus.

The Essentials of the Marxist Theory of the State

Let me first clarify one important point: the State (and its existence in its apparatus) has no meaning except as a function of *State power*. The whole of the political class struggle revolves around the State. By which I mean around the possession, i.e. the seizure and conservation of State power by a certain class or by an alliance between classes or class fractions. This first clarification obliges me to distinguish between State power (conservation of State power or seizure of State power), the objective of the political class struggle on the one hand, and the State apparatus on the other.

We know that the State apparatus may survive, as is proved by bourgeois 'revolutions' in nineteenth-century France (1830, 1848), by *coups d'état* (2 December, May 1958), by collapses of the State (the fall of the Empire in 1870, of the Third Republic in 1940), or by the political rise of the petty bourgeoisie (1890–95 in France), etc., without the State apparatus being affected or modified: it may survive political events which affect the possession of State power.

Even after a social revolution like that of 1917, a large part of the State apparatus survived after the seizure of State power by the alliance of the proletariat and the small peasantry: Lenin repeated the fact again and again.

It is possible to describe the distinction between State power and State apparatus as part of the 'Marxist theory' of the State, explicitly present since Marx's *Eighteenth Brumaire* and *Class Struggles in France*.

To summarize the 'Marxist theory of the State' on this point, it can be said that the Marxist classics have always claimed that (1) the State is the repressive State apparatus, (2) State power and State apparatus must be distinguished, (3) the objective of the class struggle concerns State power, and in consequence the use of the State apparatus by the classes (or alliance of classes or of fractions of classes) holding State power as a function of their class objectives, and (4) the proletariat must seize State power in order to destroy the existing bourgeois State apparatus and, in a first phase, replace it with a quite different, proletarian, State apparatus, then in later phases set in motion a radical process, that of the destruction of the State (the end of State power, the end of every State apparatus).

In this perspective, therefore, what I would propose to add to the 'Marxist theory' of the State is already there in so many words. But it seems to me that even with this supplement, this theory is still in part descriptive, although it does now contain complex and differential elements whose functioning and action cannot be understood without recourse to further supplementary theoretical development.

The State Ideological Apparatuses

Thus, what has to be added to the 'Marxist theory' of the State is something else.

Here we must advance cautiously in a terrain which, in fact, the Marxist classics entered long before us, but without having systematized in theoretical form the decisive advances implied by their experiences and procedures. Their experiences and procedures were indeed restricted in the main to the terrain of political practice.

In fact, i.e. in their political practice, the Marxist classics treated the State as a more complex reality than the definition of it given in the 'Marxist theory of the State', even when it has been supplemented as I have just suggested. They recognized this complexity in their practice, but they did not express it in a corresponding theory.[7]

I should like to attempt a very schematic outline of this corresponding theory. To that end, I propose the following thesis.

In order to advance the theory of the State it is indispensable to take into account not only the distinction between *State power* and *State apparatus*, but also another reality which is clearly on the side of the (repressive) State apparatus, but must not be confused with it. I shall call this reality by its concept: *the ideological State apparatuses*.

What are the ideological State apparatuses (ISAs)?

They must not be confused with the (repressive) State apparatus. Remember that in Marxist theory, the State Apparatus (SA) contains: the Government, the Admin-

7. To my knowledge, Gramsci is the only one who went any distance in the road I am taking. He had the 'remarkable' idea that the State could not be reduced to the (Repressive) State Apparatus, but included, as he put it, a certain number of institutions from '*civil society*': the Church, the Schools, the trade unions, etc. Unfortunately, Gramsci did not systematize his institutions, which remained in the state of acute but fragmentary notes (cf. Gramsci, *Selections from the Prison Notebooks*, International Publishers, 1971, pp. 12, 259, 260-3; see also the letter to Tatiana Schucht, 7 September 1931, in *Lettre del Carcere*, Einaudi, 1968, p. 479. English-language translation in preparation.

istration, the Army, the Police, the Courts, the Prisons, etc., which constitute what I shall in future call the Repressive State Apparatus. Repressive suggests that the State Apparatus in question 'functions by violence' – at least ultimately (since repression, e.g. administrative repression, may take non-physical forms).

I shall call Ideological State Apparatuses a certain number of realities which present themselves to the immediate observer in the form of distinct and specialized institutions. I propose an empirical list of these which will obviously have to be examined in detail, tested, corrected and re-organized. With all the reservations implied by this requirement, we can for the moment regard the following institutions as Ideological State Apparatuses (the order in which I have listed them has no particular significance):

- the religious ISA (the system of the different Churches),
- the educational ISA (the system of the different public and private 'Schools'),
- the family ISA,[8]
- the legal ISA,[9]
- the political ISA (the political system, including the different Parties),
- the trade-union ISA,
- the communications ISA (press, radio and television, etc.),
- the cultural ISA (Literature, the Arts, sports, etc.).

I have said that the ISAs must not be confused with the (Repressive) State Apparatus. What constitutes the difference?

8. The family obviously has other 'functions' than that of an ISA. It intervenes in the reproduction of labour power. In different modes of production it is the unit of production and/or the unit of consumption.

9. The 'Law' belongs both to the (Repressive) State Apparatus and to the system of the ISAs.

As a first moment, it is clear that while there is *one* (Repressive) State Apparatus, there is a *plurality* of Ideological State Apparatuses. Even presupposing that it exists, the unity that constitutes this plurality of ISAs as a body is not immediately visible.

As a second moment, it is clear that whereas the – unified – (Repressive) State Apparatus belongs entirely to the *public* domain, much the larger part of the Ideological State Apparatuses (in their apparent dispersion) are part, on the contrary, of the *private* domain. Churches, Parties, Trade Unions, families, some schools, most newspapers, cultural ventures, etc., etc., are private.

We can ignore the first observation for the moment. But someone is bound to question the second, asking me by what right I regard as Ideological *State* Apparatuses, institutions which for the most part do not possess public status, but are quite simply *private* institutions. As a conscious Marxist, Gramsci already forestalled this objection in one sentence. The distinction between the public and the private is a distinction internal to bourgeois law, and valid in the (subordinate) domains in which bourgeois law exercises its 'authority'. The domain of the State escapes it because the latter is 'above the law': the State, which is the State *of* the ruling class, is neither public nor private; on the contrary, it is the precondition for any distinction between public and private. The same thing can be said from the starting-point of our State Ideological Apparatuses. It is unimportant whether the institutions in which they are realized are 'public' or 'private'. What matters is how they function. Private institutions can perfectly well 'function' as Ideological State Apparatuses. A reasonably thorough analysis of any one of the ISAs proves it.

But now for what is essential. What distinguishes the ISAs from the (Repressive) State Apparatus is the following basic difference: the Repressive State Apparatus functions 'by violence', whereas the Ideological State Apparatuses *function 'by ideology'*.

I can clarify matters by correcting this distinction. I shall say rather that every State Apparatus, whether Repressive or Ideological, 'functions' both by violence and by ideology, but with one very important distinction which makes it imperative not to confuse the Ideological State Apparatuses with the (Repressive) State Apparatus.

This is the fact that the (Repressive) State Apparatus functions massively and predominantly *by repression* (including physical repression), while functioning secondarily by ideology. (There is no such thing as a purely repressive apparatus.) For example, the Army and the Police also function by ideology both to ensure their own cohesion and reproduction, and in the 'values' they propound externally.

In the same way, but inversely, it is essential to say that for their part the Ideological State Apparatuses function massively and predominantly *by ideology*, but they also function secondarily by repression, even if ultimately, but only ultimately, this is very attentuated and concealed, even symbolic. (There is no such thing as a purely ideological apparatus.) Thus Schools and Churches use suitable methods of punishment, expulsion, selection, etc., to 'discipline' not only their shepherds, but also their flocks. The same is true of the Family. . . . The same is true of the cultural IS Apparatus (censorship, among other things), etc.

Is it necessary to add that this determination of the double 'functioning' (predominantly, secondarily) by repression and by ideology, according to whether it is a matter of the (Repressive) State Apparatus or the Ideological State Apparatuses, makes it clear that very subtle explicit or tacit combinations may be woven from the interplay of the (Repressive) State Apparatus and the Ideological State Apparatuses? Everyday life provides us with innumerable examples of this, but they must be studied in detail if we are to go further than this mere observation.

Nevertheless, this remark leads us towards an understanding of what constitutes the unity of the apparently disparate body of the ISAs. If the ISAs 'function' massively and predominantly by ideology, what unifies their diversity is precisely this functioning, insofar as the ideology by which they function is always in fact unified, despite ·its diversity and its contradictions, *beneath the ruling ideology*, which is the ideology of 'the ruling class'. Given the fact that the 'ruling class' in principle holds State power (openly or more often by means of alliances between classes or class fractions), and therefore has at its disposal the (Repressive) State Apparatus, we can accept the fact that this same ruling class is active in the Ideological State Apparatuses insofar as it is ultimately the ruling ideology which is realized in the Ideological State Apparatuses, precisely in its contradictions. Of course, it is a quite different thing to act by laws and decrees in the (Repressive) State Apparatus and to 'act' through the intermediary of the ruling ideology in the Ideological State Apparatuses. We must go into the details of this difference – but it cannot mask the reality of a profound identity. To my knowledge, *no class can hold State power over a long period without at the same time exercising its hegemony over and in the State Ideological Apparatuses*. I only need one example and proof of this: Lenin's anguished concern to revolutionize the educational Ideological State Apparatus (among others), simply to make it possible for the Soviet proletariat, who had seized State power, to secure the future of the dictatorship of the proletariat and the transition to socialism.[10]

10. In a pathetic text written in 1937, Krupskaya relates the history of Lenin's desperate efforts and what she regards as his failure.

This last comment puts us in a position to understand that the Ideological State Apparatuses may be not only the *stake*, but also the *site* of class struggle, and often of bitter forms of class struggle. The class (or class alliance) in power cannot lay down the law in the ISAs as easily as it can in the (repressive) State apparatus, not only because the former ruling classes are able to retain strong positions there for a long time, but also because the resistance of the exploited classes is able to find means and occasions to express itself there, either by the utilization of their contradictions, or by conquering combat positions in them in struggle.[11]

Let me run through my comments.

If the thesis I have proposed is well-founded, it leads me back to the classical Marxist theory of the State, while making it more precise in one point. I argue that it is necessary to distinguish between State power (and its possession by . . .) on the one hand, and the State Apparatus on the other. But I add that the State Apparatus contains

---

11. What I have said in these few brief words about the class struggle in the ISAs is obviously far from exhausting the question of the class struggle.

To approach this question, two principles must be borne in mind:

The first principle was formulated by Marx in the Preface to *A Contribution to the Critique of Political Economy*: 'In considering such transformations [a social revolution] a distinction should always be made between the material transformation of the economic conditions of production, which can be determined with the precision of natural science, and the legal, political, religious, aesthetic or philosophic – in short, ideological forms in which men become conscious of this conflict and fight it out.' The class struggle is thus expressed and exercised in ideological forms, thus also in the ideological forms of the ISAs. But the class struggle *extends far beyond* these forms, and it is because it extends beyond them that the struggle of the exploited classes may also be exercised in the forms of the ISAs, and thus turn the weapon of ideology against the classes in power.

This by virtue of the *second principle*: the class struggle extends beyond the ISAs because it is rooted elsewhere than in ideology, in the Infrastructure, in the relations of production, which are relations of exploitation and constitute the base for class relations.

two bodies: the body of institutions which represent the Repressive State Apparatus on the one hand, and the body of institutions which represent the body of Ideological State Apparatuses on the other.

But if this is the case, the following question is bound to be asked, even in the very summary state of my suggestions: what exactly is the extent of the role of the Ideological State Apparatuses? What is their importance based on? In other words: to what does the 'function' of these Ideological State Apparatuses, which do not function by repression but by ideology, correspond?

ON THE REPRODUCTION OF THE RELATIONS OF PRODUCTION

I can now answer the central question which I have left in suspense for many long pages: *how is the reproduction of the relations of production secured?*

In the topographical language (Infrastructure, Superstructure), I can say: for the most part,[12] it is secured by the legal-political and ideological superstructure.

But as I have argued that it is essential to go beyond this still descriptive language, I shall say: for the most part,[12] it is secured by the exercise of State power in the State Apparatuses, on the one hand the (Repressive) State Apparatus, on the other the Ideological State Apparatuses.

What I have just said must also be taken into account, and it can be assembled in the form of the following three features:

12. For the most part. For the relations of production are first reproduced by the materiality of the processes of production and circulation. But it should not be forgotten that ideological relations are immediately present in these same processes.

1. All the State Apparatuses function both by repression and by ideology, with the difference that the (Repressive) State Apparatus functions massively and predominantly by repression, whereas the Ideological State Apparatuses function massively and predominantly by ideology.

2. Whereas the (Repressive) State Apparatus constitutes an organized whole whose different parts are centralized beneath a commanding unity, that of the politics of class struggle applied by the political representatives of the ruling classes in possession of State power, the Ideological State Apparatuses are multiple, distinct, 'relatively autonomous' and capable of providing an objective field to contradictions which express, in forms which may be limited or extreme, the effects of the clashes between the capitalist class struggle and the proletarian class struggle, as well as their subordinate forms.

3. Whereas the unity of the (Repressive) State Apparatus is secured by its unified and centralized organization under the leadership of the representatives of the classes in power executing the politics of the class struggle of the classes in power, the unity of the different Ideological State Apparatuses is secured, usually in contradictory forms, by the ruling ideology, the ideology of the ruling class.

Taking these features into account, it is possible to represent the reproduction of the relations of production[13] in the following way, according to a kind of 'division of labour'.

The role of the repressive State apparatus, insofar as it is a repressive apparatus, consists essentially in securing by force (physical or otherwise) the political conditions of the reproduction of relations of production which are in the

---

13. *For that part* of reproduction to which the Repressive State Apparatus and the Ideological State Apparatus *contribute*.

last resort *relations of exploitation*. Not only does the State apparatus contribute generously to its own reproduction (the capitalist State contains political dynasties, military dynasties, etc.), but also and above all, the State apparatus secures by repression (from the most brutal physical force, via mere administrative commands and interdictions, to open and tacit censorship) the political conditions for the action of the Ideological State Apparatuses.

In fact, it is the latter which largely secure the reproduction specifically of the relations of production, behind a 'shield' provided by the repressive State apparatus. It is here that the role of the ruling ideology is heavily concentrated, the ideology of the ruling class, which holds State power. It is the intermediation of the ruling ideology that ensures a (sometimes teeth-gritting) 'harmony' between the repressive State apparatus and the Ideological State Apparatuses, and between the different State Ideological Apparatuses.

We are thus led to envisage the following hypothesis, as a function precisely of the diversity of ideological State Apparatuses in their single, because shared, role of the reproduction of the relations of production.

Indeed we have listed a relatively large number of ideological State apparatuses in contemporary capitalist social formations: the educational apparatus, the religious apparatus, the family apparatus, the political apparatus, the trade-union apparatus, the communications apparatus, the 'cultural' apparatus, etc.

But in the social formations of that mode of production characterized by 'serfdom' (usually called the feudal mode of production), we observe that although there is a single repressive State apparatus which, since the earliest known Ancient States, let alone the Absolute Monarchies, has been formally very similar to the one we know today, the number of Ideological State Apparatuses is smaller and their

individual types are different. For example, we observe that
during the Middle Ages, the Church (the religious ideological State apparatus) accumulated a number of functions
which have today devolved on to several distinct ideological
State apparatuses, new ones in relation to the past I am
invoking, in particular educational and cultural functions.
Alongside the Church there was the family Ideological State
Apparatus, which played a considerable part, incommensur-
able with its role in capitalist social formations. Despite
appearances, the Church and the Family were not the only
Ideological State Apparatuses. There was also a political
Ideological State Apparatus (the Estates General, the *Parle-
ment*, the different political factions and Leagues, the ancestors or the modern political parties, and the whole political
system of the free Communes and then of the *Villes*). There
was also a powerful 'proto-trade-union' Ideological State
Apparatus, if I may venture such an anachronistic term (the
powerful merchants' and bankers' guilds and the journey-
men's associations, etc.). Publishing and Communications,
even, saw an indisputable development, as did the theatre;
initially both were integral parts of the Church, then they
became more and more independent of it.

In the pre-capitalist historical period which I have
examined extremely broadly, it is absolutely clear that
*there was one dominant Ideological State Apparatus, the
Church*, which concentrated within it not only religious
functions, but also educational ones, and a large proportion
of the functions of communications and 'culture'. It is no
accident that all ideological struggle, from the sixteenth
to the eighteenth century, starting with the first shocks of
the Reformation, was *concentrated* in an anti-clerical and
anti-religious struggle; rather this is a function precisely
of the dominant position of the religious ideological State
apparatus.

The foremost objective and achievement of the French

Revolution was not just to transfer State power from the feudal aristocracy to the merchant-capitalist bourgeoisie, to break part of the former repressive State apparatus and replace it with a new one (e.g., the national popular Army) – but also to attack the number-one Ideological State Apparatus: the Church. Hence the civil constitution of the clergy, the confiscation of ecclesiastical wealth, and the creation of new ideological State apparatuses to replace the religious ideological State apparatus in its dominant role.

Naturally, these things did not happen automatically: witness the Concordat, the Restoration and the long class struggle between the landed aristocracy and the industrial bourgeoisie throughout the nineteenth century for the establishment of bourgeois hegemony over the functions formerly fulfilled by the Church: above all by the Schools. It can be said that the bourgeoisie relied on the new political, parliamentary-democratic, ideological State apparatus, installed in the earliest years of the Revolution, then restored after long and violent struggles, for a few months in 1848 and for decades after the fall of the Second Empire, in order to conduct its struggle against the Church and wrest its ideological functions away from it, in other words, to ensure not only its own political hegemony, but also the ideological hegemony indispensable to the reproduction of capitalist relations of production.

That is why I believe that I am justified in advancing the following Thesis, however precarious it is. I believe that the ideological State apparatus which has been installed in the *dominant* position in mature capitalist social formations as a result of a violent political and ideological class struggle against the old dominant ideological State apparatus, is the *educational ideological apparatus.*

This thesis may seem paradoxical, given that for everyone, i.e. in the ideological representation that the bourgeoisie has tried to give itself and the classes it exploits, it really seems that the dominant ideological State apparatus in capitalist social formations is not the Schools, but the political ideological State apparatus, i.e. the regime of parliamentary democracy combining universal suffrage and party struggle.

However, history, even recent history, shows that the bourgeoisie has been and still is able to accommodate itself to political ideological State apparatuses other than parliamentary democracy: the First and Second Empires, Constitutional Monarchy (Louis XVIII and Charles X), Parliamentary Monarchy (Louis-Philippe), Presidential Democracy (de Gaulle), to mention only France. In England this is even clearer. The Revolution was particularly 'successful' there from the bourgeois point of view, since unlike France, where the bourgeoisie, partly because of the stupidity of the petty aristocracy, had to agree to being carried to power by peasant and plebeian *'journées révolutionnaires'*, something for which it had to pay a high price, the English bourgeoisie was able to 'compromise' with the aristocracy and 'share' State power and the use of the State apparatus with it for a long time (peace among all men of good will in the ruling classes!). In Germany it is even more striking, since it was behind a political ideological State apparatus in which the imperial Junkers (epitomized by Bismarck), their army and their police provided it with a shield and leading personnel, that the imperialist bourgeoisie made its shattering entry into history, before 'traversing' the Weimar Republic and entrusting itself to Nazism.

Hence I believe I have good reasons for thinking that behind the scenes of its political Ideological State Apparatus, which occupies the front of the stage, what the bourgeoisie has installed as its number-one, i.e. as its dominant ideological State apparatus, is the educational apparatus, which has in fact replaced in its functions the previously dominant ideological State apparatus, the Church. One might even add: the School-Family couple has replaced the Church-Family couple.

Why is the educational apparatus in fact the dominant ideological State apparatus in capitalist social formations, and how does it function?

For the moment it must suffice to say:

1. All ideological State apparatuses, whatever they are, contribute to the same result: the reproduction of the relations of production, i.e. of capitalist relations of exploitation.

2. Each of them contributes towards this single result in the way proper to it. The political apparatus by subjecting individuals to the political State ideology, the 'indirect' (parliamentary) or 'direct' (plebiscitary or fascist) 'democratic' ideology. The communications apparatus by cramming every 'citizen' with daily doses of nationalism, chauvinism, liberalism, moralism, etc, by means of the press, the radio and television. The same goes for the cultural apparatus (the role of sport in chauvinism is of the first importance), etc. The religious apparatus by recalling in sermons and the other great ceremonies of Birth, Marriage and Death, that man is only ashes, unless he loves his neighbour to the extent of turning the other cheek to whoever strikes first. The family apparatus ... but there is no need to go on.

3. This concert is dominated by a single score, occasionally disturbed by contradictions (those of the remnants of former ruling classes, those of the proletarians and their organizations): the score of the Ideology of the current ruling class which integrates into its music the great themes of the Humanism of the Great Forefathers, who produced the Greek Miracle even before Christianity, and afterwards

the Glory of Rome, the Eternal City, and the themes of Interest, particular and general, etc. nationalism, moralism and economism.

4. Nevertheless, in this concert, one ideological State apparatus certainly has the dominant role, although hardly anyone lends an ear to its music: it is so silent! This is the School.

It takes children from every class at infant-school age, and then for years, the years in which the child is most 'vulnerable', squeezed between the family State apparatus and the educational State apparatus, it drums into them, whether it uses new or old methods, a certain amount of 'know-how' wrapped in the ruling ideology (French, arithmetic, natural history, the sciences, literature) or simply the ruling ideology in its pure state (ethics, civic instruction, philosophy). Somewhere around the age of sixteen, a huge mass of children are ejected 'into production': these are the workers or small peasants. Another portion of scholastically adapted youth carries on: and, for better or worse, it goes somewhat further, until it falls by the wayside and fills the posts of small and middle technicians, white-collar workers, small and middle executives, petty bourgeois of all kinds. A last portion reaches the summit, either to fall into intellectual semi-employment, or to provide, as well as the 'intellectuals of the collective labourer', the agents of exploitation (capitalists, managers), the agents of repression (soldiers, policemen, politicians, administrators, etc.) and the professional ideologists (priests of all sorts, most of whom are convinced 'laymen').

Each mass ejected *en route* is practically provided with the ideology which suits the role it has to fulfil in class society: the role of the exploited (with a 'highly-developed' 'professional', 'ethical', 'civic', 'national' and a-political consciousness); the role of the agent of exploitation (ability to give the workers orders and speak to them: 'human relations'), of the agent of repression (ability to give orders and enforce obedience 'without discussion', or ability to manipulate the demagogy of a political leader's rhetoric), or of the professional ideologist (ability to treat consciousnesses with the respect, i.e. with the contempt, blackmail, and demagogy they deserve, adapted to the accents of Morality, of Virtue, of 'Transcendence', of the Nation, of France's World Role, etc.).

Of course, many of these contrasting Virtues (modesty, resignation, submissiveness on the one hand, cynicism, contempt, arrogance, confidence, self-importance, even smooth talk and cunning on the other) are also taught in the Family, in the Church, in the Army, in Good Books, in films and even in the football stadium. But no other ideological State apparatus has the obligatory (and not least, free) audience of the totality of the children in the capitalist social formation, eight hours a day for five or six days out of seven.

But it is by an apprenticeship in a variety of know-how wrapped up in the massive inculcation of the ideology of the ruling class that the *relations of production* in a capitalist social formation, i.e. the relations of exploited to exploiters and exploiters to exploited, are largely reproduced. The mechanisms which produce this vital result for the capitalist regime are naturally covered up and concealed by a universally reigning ideology of the School, universally reigning because it is one of the essential forms of the ruling bourgeois ideology: an ideology which represents the School as a neutral environment purged of ideology (because it is . . . lay), where teachers respectful of the 'conscience' and 'freedom' of the children who are entrusted to them (in complete confidence) by their 'parents' (who are free, too, i.e. the owners of their children) open up for them the path to the freedom, morality and responsibility of adults by their own example, by knowledge, literature and their 'liberating' virtues.

I ask the pardon of those teachers who, in dreadful conditions, attempt to turn the few weapons they can find in the history and learning they 'teach' against the ideology, the system and the practices in which they are trapped. They are a kind of hero. But they are rare and how many (the majority) do not even begin to suspect the 'work' the system (which is bigger than they are and crushes them) forces them to do, or worse, put all their heart and ingenuity into performing it with the most advanced awareness (the famous new methods!). So little do they suspect it that their own devotion contributes to the maintenance and nourishment of this ideological representation of the School, which makes the School today as 'natural', indispensable-useful and even beneficial for our contemporaries as the Church was 'natural', indispensable and generous for our ancestors a few centuries ago.

In fact, the Church has been replaced today *in its role as the dominant Ideological State Apparatus* by the School. It is coupled with the Family just as the Church was once coupled with the Family. We can now claim that the unprecedentedly deep crisis which is now shaking the education system of so many States across the globe, often in conjunction with a crisis (already proclaimed in the *Communist Manifesto*) shaking the family system, takes on a political meaning, given that the School (and the School-Family couple) constitutes the dominant Ideological State Apparatus, the Apparatus playing a determinant part in the reproduction of the relations of production of a mode of production threatened in its existence by the world class struggle.

ON IDEOLOGY

When I put forward the concept of an Ideological State
Apparatus, when I said that the ISAs 'function by ideology',
I invoked a reality which needs a little discussion: ideology.

It is well known that the expression 'ideology' was in-
vented by Cabanis, Destutt de Tracy and their friends, who
assigned to it as an object the (genetic) theory of ideas. When
Marx took up the term fifty years later, he gave it a quite
different meaning, even in his Early Works. Here, ideology
is the system of the ideas and representations which dominate the mind of a man or a social group. The ideologico-
political struggle conducted by Marx as early as his articles
in the *Rheinische Zeitung* inevitably and quickly brought
him face to face with this reality and forced him to take his
earliest intuitions further.

However, here we come upon a rather astonishing paradox. Everything seems to lead Marx to formulate a theory
of ideology. In fact, *The German Ideology* does offer us,
after the *1844 Manuscripts*, an explicit theory of ideology,
but . . . it is not Marxist (we shall see why in a moment).
As for *Capital*, although it does contain many hints towards
a theory of ideologies (most visibly, the ideology of the
vulgar economists), it does not contain that theory itself,
which depends for the most part on a theory of ideology in
general.

I should like to venture a first and very schematic outline
of such a theory. The theses I am about to put forward are
certainly not off the cuff, but they cannot be sustained and
tested, i.e. confirmed or rejected, except by much thorough
study and analysis.

Ideology has no History

One word first of all to expound the reason in principle which seems to me to found, or at least to justify, the project of a theory of ideology *in general*, and not a theory of particular ideolog*ies*, which, whatever their form (religious, ethical, legal, political), always express *class positions*.

It is quite obvious that it is necessary to proceed towards a theory of ideolog*ies* in the two respects I have just suggested. It will then be clear that a theory of ideolog*ies* depends in the last resort on the history of social formations, and thus of the modes of production combined in social formations, and of the class struggles which develop in them. In this sense it is clear that there can be no question of a theory of ideolog*ies in general*, since ideolog*ies* (defined in the double respect suggested above: regional and class) have a history, whose determination in the last instance is clearly situated outside ideologies alone, although it involves them.

On the contrary, if I am able to put forward the project of a theory of ideology *in general*, and if this theory really is one of the elements on which theories of ideolog*ies* depend, that entails an apparently paradoxical proposition which I shall express in the following terms: *ideology has no history*.

As we know, this formulation appears in so many words in a passage from *The German Ideology*. Marx utters it with respect to metaphysics, which, he says, has no more history than ethics (meaning also the other forms of ideology).

In *The German Ideology*, this formulation appears in a plainly positivist context. Ideology is conceived as a pure illusion, a pure dream, i.e. as nothingness. All its reality is external to it. Ideology is thus thought as an imaginary construction whose status is exactly like the theoretical status of the dream among writers before Freud. For these writers, the dream was the purely imaginary, i.e. null, result of 'day's residues', presented in an arbitrary arrangement and order, sometimes even 'inverted', in other words, in 'disorder'. For them, the dream was the imaginary, it was empty, null and arbitrarily 'stuck together' (*bricolé*), once the eyes had closed, from the residues of the only full and positive reality, the reality of the day. This is exactly the status of philosophy and ideology (since in this book philosophy is ideology *par excellence*) in *The German Ideology*.

Ideology, then, is for Marx an imaginary assemblage (*bricolage*), a pure dream, empty and vain, constituted by the 'day's residues' from the only full and positive reality, that of the concrete history of concrete material individuals materially producing their existence. It is on this basis that ideology has no history in *The German Ideology*, since its history is outside it, where the only existing history is, the history of concrete individuals, etc. In *The German Ideology*, the thesis that ideology has no history is therefore a purely negative thesis, since it means both:

1. ideology is nothing insofar as it is a pure dream (manufactured by who knows what power: if not by the alienation of the division of labour, but that, too, is a *negative* determination);

2. ideology has no history, which emphatically does not mean that there is no history in it (on the contrary, for it is merely the pale, empty and inverted reflection of real history) but that it has no history *of its own*.

Now, while the thesis I wish to defend formally speaking adopts the terms of *The German Ideology* ('ideology has no history'), it is radically different from the positivist and historicist thesis of *The German Ideology*.

For on the one hand, I think it is possible to hold that ideolog*ies have a history of their own* (although it is determined in the last instance by the class struggle); and on the other, I think it is possible to hold that ideology *in general* *has no history*, not in a negative sense (its history is external to it), but in an absolutely positive sense.

This sense is a positive one if it is true that the peculiarity of ideology is that it is endowed with a structure and a functioning such as to make it a non-historical reality, i.e. an *omni-historical* reality, in the sense in which that structure and functioning are immutable, present in the same form throughout what we can call history, in the sense in which the *Communist Manifesto* defines history as the history of class struggles, i.e. the history of class societies.

To give a theoretical reference-point here, I might say that, to return to our example of the dream, in its Freudian conception this time, our proposition: ideology has no history, can and must (and in a way which has absolutely nothing arbitrary about it, but, quite the reverse, is theoretically necessary, for there is an organic link between the two propositions) be related directly to Freud's proposition that the *unconscious is eternal,* i.e. that it has no history.

If eternal means, not transcendent to all (temporal) history, but omnipresent, trans-historical and therefore immutable in form throughout the extent of history, I shall adopt Freud's expression word for word, and write *ideology is eternal*, exactly like the unconscious. And I add that I find this comparison theoretically justified by the fact that the eternity of the unconscious is not unrelated to the eternity of ideology in general.

That is why I believe I am justified, hypothetically at least, in proposing a theory of ideology *in general*, in the sense that Freud presented a theory of the unconscious *in general*.

To simplify the phrase, it is convenient, taking into account what has been said about ideologies, to use the plain term ideology to designate ideology in general, which I have just said has no history, or, what comes to the same thing, is eternal, i.e. omnipresent in its immutable form throughout history (= the history of social formations containing social classes). For the moment I shall restrict myself to 'class societies' and their history.

Ideology is a 'Representation' of the Imaginary Relationship of Individuals to their Real Conditions of Existence

In order to approach my central thesis on the structure and functioning of ideology, I shall first present two theses, one negative, the other positive. The first concerns the object which is 'represented' in the imaginary form of ideology, the second concerns the materiality of ideology.

THESIS I: Ideology represents the imaginary relationship of individuals to their real conditions of existence.

We commonly call religious ideology, ethical ideology, legal ideology, political ideology, etc., so many 'world outlooks'. Of course, assuming that we do not live one of these ideologies as the truth (e.g. 'believe' in God, Duty, Justice, etc. . . .), we admit that the ideology we are discussing from a critical point of view, examining it as the ethnologist examines the myths of a 'primitive society', that these 'world outlooks' are largely imaginary, i.e. do not 'correspond to reality'.

However, while admitting that they do not correspond to reality, i.e. that they constitute an illusion, we admit that they do make allusion to reality, and that they need only be 'interpreted' to discover the reality of the world behind their imaginary representation of that world (ideology = *illusion/allusion*).

There are different types of interpretation, the most famous of which are the *mechanistic* type, current in the eighteenth century (God is the imaginary representation of the real King), and the '*hermeneutic*' interpretation, inaugurated by the earliest Church Fathers, and revived by

Feuerbach and the theologico-philosophical school which descends from him, e.g. the theologian Barth (to Feuerbach, for example, God is the essence of real Man). The essential point is that on condition that we interpret the imaginary transposition (and inversion) of ideology we arrive at the conclusion that in ideology 'men represent their real conditions of existence to themselves in an imaginary form'.

Unfortunately, this interpretation leaves one small problem unsettled: why do men 'need' this imaginary transposition of their real conditions of existence in order to 'represent to themselves' their real conditions of existence?

The first answer (that of the eighteenth century) proposes a simple solution: Priests or Despots are responsible. They 'forged' the Beautiful Lies so that, in the belief that they were obeying God, men would in fact obey the Priests and Despots, who are usually in alliance in their imposture, the Priests acting in the interests of the Despots or *vice versa*, according to the political positions of the 'theoreticians' concerned. There is therefore a cause for the imaginary transposition of the real conditions of existence: that cause is the existence of a small number of cynical men who base their domination and exploitation of the 'people' on a falsified representation of the world which they have imagined in order to enslave other minds by dominating their imaginations.

The second answer (that of Feuerbach, taken over word for word by Marx in his Early Works) is more 'profound', i.e. just as false. It, too, seeks and finds a cause for the imaginary transposition and distortion of men's real conditions of existence, in short, for the alienation in the imaginary of the representation of men's conditions of existence. This cause is no longer Priests or Despots, nor their active imagination and the passive imagination of their victims. This cause is the material alienation which reigns in the conditions of existence of men themselves. This is how, in *The Jewish Question* and elsewhere, Marx defends the Feuerbachian idea that men make themselves an alienated (= imaginary) representation of their conditions of existence because these conditions of existence are themselves alienating (in the *1844 Manuscripts*: because these conditions are dominated by the essence of alienated society – '*alienated labour*').

All these interpretations thus take literally the thesis which they presuppose, and on which they depend, i.e. that what is reflected in the imaginary representation of the world found in an ideology is the conditions of existence of men, i.e. their real world.

Now I can return to a thesis which I have already advanced: it is not their real conditions of existence, their real world, that 'men' 'represent to themselves' in ideology, but above all it is their relation to those conditions of existence which is represented to them there. It is this relation which is at the centre of every ideological, i.e. imaginary, representation of the real world. It is this relation that contains the 'cause' which has to explain the imaginary distortion of the ideological representation of the real world. Or rather, to leave aside the language of causality it is necessary to advance the thesis that it is the *imaginary nature of this relation* which underlies all the imaginary distortion that we can observe (if we do not live in its truth) in all ideology.

To speak in a Marxist language, if it is true that the representation of the real conditions of existence of the individuals occupying the posts of agents of production, exploitation, repression, ideologization and scientific practice, does in the last analysis arise from the relations of production, and from relations deriving from the relations of production, we can say the following: all ideology represents in its necessarily imaginary distortion not the existing relations of production (and the other relations that derive from them), but above all the (imaginary) relationship of individuals to the relations of production and the relations that derive from them. What is represented in ideology is therefore not the system of the real relations which govern the existence of individuals, but the imaginary relation of those individuals to the real relations in which they live.

If this is the case, the question of the 'cause' of the imaginary distortion of the real relations in ideology disappears and must be replaced by a different question: why is the representation given to individuals of their (individual) relation to the social relations which govern their conditions of existence and their collective and individual life necessarily an imaginary relation? And what is the nature of this imaginariness? Posed in this way, the question explodes the solution by a 'clique'[14], by a group of individuals (Priests or Despots) who are the authors of the great ideological mystification, just as it explodes the solution by the alienated character of the real world. We shall see why later in my exposition. For the moment I shall go no further.

THESIS II: Ideology has a material existence.

I have already touched on this thesis by saying that the 'ideas' or 'representations', etc., which seem to make up ideology do not have an ideal (*idéale* or *idéelle*) or spiritual existence, but a material existence. I even suggested that the ideal (*idéale*, *idéelle*) and spiritual existence of 'ideas' arises exclusively in an ideology of the 'idea' and of ideology, and let me add, in an ideology of what seems to have 'founded' this conception since the emergence of the sciences, i.e. what

14. I use this very modern term deliberately. For even in Communist circles, unfortunately, it is a commonplace to 'explain' some political deviation (left or right opportunism) by the action of a 'clique'.

the practicians of the sciences represent to themselves in their spontaneous ideology as 'ideas', true or false. Of course, presented in affirmative form, this thesis is unproven. I simply ask that the reader be favourably disposed towards it, say, in the name of materialism. A long series of arguments would be necessary to prove it.

This hypothetical thesis of the not spiritual but material existence of 'ideas' or other 'representations' is indeed necessary if we are to advance in our analysis of the nature of ideology. Or rather, it is merely useful to us in order the better to reveal what every at all serious analysis of any ideology will immediately and empirically show to every observer, however critical.

While discussing the ideological State apparatuses and their practices, I said that each of them was the realization of an ideology (the unity of these different regional ideologies – religious, ethical, legal, political, aesthetic, etc. – being assured by their subjection to the ruling ideology). I now return to this thesis: an ideology always exists in an apparatus, and its practice, or practices. This existence is material.

Of course, the material existence of the ideology in an apparatus and its practices does not have the same modality as the material existence of a paving-stone or a rifle. But, at the risk of being taken for a Neo-Aristotelian (NB Marx had a very high regard for Aristotle), I shall say that 'matter is discussed in many senses', or rather that it exists in different modalities, all rooted in the last instance in 'physical' matter.

Having said this, let me move straight on and see what happens to the 'individuals' who live in ideology, i.e. in a determinate (religious, ethical, etc.) representation of the world whose imaginary distortion depends on their imaginary relation to their conditions of existence, in other words, in the last instance, to the relations of production and to class relations (ideology = an imaginary relation to real relations). I shall say that this imaginary relation is itself endowed with a material existence.

Now I observe the following.

An individual believes in God, or Duty, or Justice, etc. This belief derives (for everyone, i.e. for all those who live in an ideological representation of ideology, which reduces ideology to ideas endowed by definition with a spiritual existence) from the ideas of the individual concerned, i.e. from him as a subject with a consciousness which contains the ideas of his belief. In this way, i.e. by means of the absolutely ideological 'conceptual' device (*dispositif*) thus set up (a subject endowed with a consciousness in which he freely forms or freely recognizes ideas in which he believes), the (material) attitude of the subject concerned naturally follows.

The individual in question behaves in such and such a way, adopts such and such a practical attitude, and, what is more, participates in certain regular practices which are those of the ideological apparatus on which 'depend' the ideas which he has in all consciousness freely chosen as a subject. If he believes in God, he goes to Church to attend Mass, kneels, prays, confesses, does penance (once it was material in the ordinary sense of the term) and naturally repents and so on. If he believes in Duty, he will have the corresponding attitudes, inscribed in ritual practices 'according to the correct principles'. If he believes in Justice, he will submit unconditionally to the rules of the Law, and may even protest when they are violated, sign petitions, take part in a demonstration, etc.

Throughout this schema we observe that the ideological representation of ideology is itself forced to recognize that every 'subject' endowed with a 'consciousness' and believing in the 'ideas' that his 'consciousness' inspires in him and freely accepts, must '*act* according to his ideas', must therefore inscribe his own ideas as a free subject in the actions of his material practice. If he does not do so, 'that is wicked'.

Indeed, if he does not do what he ought to do as a function of what he believes, it is because he does something else, which, still as a function of the same idealist scheme, implies that he has other ideas in his head as well as those he proclaims, and that he acts according to these other ideas, as a man who is either 'inconsistent' ('no one is willingly evil') or cynical, or perverse.

In every case, the ideology of ideology thus recognizes, despite its imaginary distortion, that the 'ideas' of a human subject exist in his actions, or ought to exist in his actions, and if that is not the case, it lends him other ideas corresponding to the actions (however perverse) that he does perform. This ideology talks of actions: I shall talk of actions inserted into *practices*. *And* I shall point out that these practices are governed by the *rituals* in which these practices are inscribed, within the *material existence of an ideological apparatus*, be it only a small part of that apparatus: a small mass in a small church, a funeral, a minor match at a sports' club, a school day, a political party meeting, etc.

Besides, we are indebted to Pascal's defensive 'dialectic' for the wonderful formula which will enable us to invert the order of the notional schema of ideology. Pascal says more or less: 'Kneel down, move your lips in prayer, and you will believe.' He thus scandalously inverts the order of things, bringing, like Christ, not peace but strife, and in addition something hardly Christian (for woe to him who brings scandal into the world!) – scandal itself. A fortunate scandal which makes him stick with Jansenist defiance to a language that directly names the reality.

I will be allowed to leave Pascal to the arguments of his

ideological struggle with the religious ideological State apparatus of his day. And I shall be expected to use a more directly Marxist vocabulary, if that is possible, for we are advancing in still poorly explored domains.

I shall therefore say that, where only a single subject (such and such an individual) is concerned, the existence of the ideas of his belief is material in that *his ideas are his material actions inserted into material practices governed by material rituals which are themselves defined by the material ideological apparatus from which derive the ideas of that subject.* Naturally, the four inscriptions of the adjective 'material' in my proposition must be affected by different modalities: the materialities of a displacement for going to mass, of kneeling down, of the gesture of the sign of the cross, or of the *mea culpa*, of a sentence, of a prayer, of an act of contrition, of a penitence, of a gaze, of a hand-shake, of an external verbal discourse or an 'internal' verbal discourse (consciousness), are not one and the same materiality. I shall leave on one side the problem of a theory of the differences between the modalities of materiality.

It remains that in this inverted presentation of things, we are not dealing with an 'inversion' at all, since it is clear that certain notions have purely and simply disappeared from our presentation, whereas others on the contrary survive, and new terms appear.

Disappeared: the term *ideas*.

Survive: the terms *subject, consciousness, belief, actions*.

Appear: the terms *practices, rituals, ideological apparatus*.

It is therefore not an inversion or overturning (except in the sense in which one might say a government or a glass is overturned), but a reshuffle (of a non-ministerial type), a rather strange reshuffle, since we obtain the following result.

Ideas have disappeared as such (insofar as they are endowed with an ideal or spiritual existence), to the precise extent that it has emerged that their existence is inscribed in the actions of practices governed by rituals defined in the last instance by an ideological apparatus. It therefore appears that the subject acts insofar as he is acted by the following system (set out in the order of its real determination): ideology existing in a material ideological apparatus, prescribing material practices governed by a material ritual, which practices exist in the material actions of a subject acting in all consciousness according to his belief.

But this very presentation reveals that we have retained the following notions: subject, consciousness, belief, actions. From this series I shall immediately extract the decisive central term on which everything else depends: the notion of the *subject*.

And I shall immediately set down two conjoint theses:

1. there is no practice except by and in an ideology;
2. there is no ideology except by the subject and for subjects.

I can now come to my central thesis.

Ideology Interpellates Individuals as Subjects

This thesis is simply a matter of making my last proposition explicit: there is no ideology except by the subject and for subjects. Meaning, there is no ideology except for concrete subjects, and this destination for ideology is only made possible by the subject: meaning, *by the category of the subject* and its functioning.

By this I mean that, even if it only appears under this name (the subject) with the rise of bourgeois ideology, above all with the rise of legal ideology,[15] the category of the

15. Which borrowed the legal category of 'subject in law' to make an ideological notion: man is by nature a subject.

subject (which may function under other names: e.g., as the soul in Plato, as God, etc.) is the constitutive category of all ideology, whatever its determination (regional or class) and whatever its historical date – since ideology has no history.

I say: the category of the subject is constitutive of all ideology, but at the same time and immediately I add that *the category of the subject is only constitutive of all ideology insofar as all ideology has the function (which defines it) of 'constituting' concrete individuals as subjects.* In the inter-action of this double constitution exists the functioning of all ideology, ideology being nothing but its functioning in the material forms of existence of that functioning.

In order to grasp what follows, it is essential to realize that both he who is writing these lines and the reader who reads them are themselves subjects, and therefore ideologi-cal subjects (a tautological proposition), i.e. that the author and the reader of these lines both live 'spontaneously' or 'naturally' in ideology in the sense in which I have said that 'man is an ideological animal by nature'.

That the author, insofar as he writes the lines of a dis-course which claims to be scientific, is completely absent as a 'subject' from 'his' scientific discourse (for all scientific discourse is by definition a subject-less discourse, there is no 'Subject of science' except in an ideology of science) is a different question which I shall leave on one side for the moment.

As St Paul admirably put it, it is in the 'Logos', meaning in ideology, that we 'live, move and have our being'. It follows that, for you and for me, the category of the subject is a primary 'obviousness' (obviousnesses are always primary): it is clear that you and I are subjects (free, ethical, etc. . . .). Like all obviousnesses, including those that make a word 'name a thing' or 'have a meaning' (therefore including the obviousness of the 'transparency' of language), the 'obviousness' that you and I are subjects – and that that does not cause any problems – is an ideological effect, the elementary ideological effect.[16] It is indeed a peculiarity of ideology that it imposes (without appearing to do so, since these are 'obviousnesses') obviousnesses as obviousnesses, which we cannot *fail to recognize* and before which we have the inevitable and natural reaction of crying out (aloud or in the 'still, small voice of conscience'): 'That's obvious! That's right! That's true!'

At work in this reaction is the ideological *recognition* function which is one of the two functions of ideology as such (its inverse being the function of *misrecognition – méconnaissance*).

To take a highly 'concrete' example, we all have friends who, when they knock on our door and we ask, through the door, the question 'Who's there?', answer (since 'it's obvious') 'It's me'. And we recognize that 'it is him', or 'her'. We open the door, and 'it's true, it really was she who was there'. To take another example, when we recognize some-body of our (previous) acquaintance ((*re*)-*connaissance*) in the street, we show him that we have recognized him (and have recognized that he has recognized us) by saying to him 'Hello, my friend', and shaking his hand (a material ritual practice of ideological recognition in everyday life – in France, at least; elsewhere, there are other rituals).

In this preliminary remark and these concrete illustra-tions, I only wish to point out that you and I are *always already* subjects, and as such constantly practice the rituals of ideological recognition, which guarantee for us that we

16. Linguists and those who appeal to linguistics for various purposes often run up against difficulties which arise because they ignore the action of the ideological effects in all discourses – including even scientific discourses.

are indeed concrete, individual, distinguishable and (naturally) irreplaceable subjects. The writing I am currently executing and the reading you are currently[17] performing are also in this respect rituals of ideological recognition, including the 'obviousness' with which the 'truth' or 'error' of my reflections may impose itself on you.

But to recognize that we are subjects and that we function in the practical rituals of the most elementary everyday life (the hand-shake, the fact of calling you by your name, the fact of knowing, even if I do not know what it is, that you 'have' a name of your own, which means that you are recognized as a unique subject, etc.) – this recognition only gives us the 'consciousness' of our incessant (eternal) practice of ideological recognition – its consciousness, i.e. its *recognition* – but in no sense does it give us the (scientific) *knowledge* of the mechanism of this recognition. Now it is this knowledge that we have to reach, if you will, while speaking in ideology, and from within ideology we have to outline a discourse which tries to break with ideology, in order to dare to be the beginning of a scientific (i.e. subject-less) discourse on ideology.

Thus in order to represent why the category of the 'subject' is constitutive of ideology, which only exists by constituting concrete subjects as subjects, I shall employ a special mode of exposition: 'concrete' enough to be recognized, but abstract enough to be thinkable and thought, giving rise to a knowledge.

As a first formulation I shall say: *all ideology hails or interpellates concrete individuals as concrete subjects*, by the functioning of the category of the subject.

17. NB: this double 'currently' is one more proof of the fact that ideology is 'eternal', since these two 'currentlys' are separated by an indefinite interval; I am writing these lines on 6 April 1969, you may read them at any subsequent time.

This is a proposition which entails that we distinguish for the moment between concrete individuals on the one hand and concrete subjects on the other, although at this level concrete subjects only exist insofar as they are supported by a concrete individual.

I shall then suggest that ideology 'acts' or 'functions' in such a way that it 'recruits' subjects among the individuals (it recruits them all), or 'transforms' the individuals into subjects (it transforms them all) by that very precise operation which I have called *interpellation* or hailing, and which can be imagined along the lines of the most commonplace everyday police (or other) hailing: 'Hey, you there!'[18]

Assuming that the theoretical scene I have imagined takes place in the street, the hailed individual will turn round. By this mere one-hundred-and-eighty-degree physical conversion, he becomes a *subject*. Why? Because he has recognized that the hail was 'really' addressed to him, and that 'it was *really him* who was hailed' (and not someone else). Experience shows that the practical telecommunication of hailings is such that they hardly ever miss their man: verbal call or whistle, the one hailed always recognizes that it is really him who is being hailed. And yet it is a strange phenomenon, and one which cannot be explained solely by 'guilt feelings', despite the large numbers who 'have something on their consciences'.

Naturally for the convenience and clarity of my little theoretical theatre I have had to present things in the form of a sequence, with a before and an after, and thus in the form of a temporal succession. There are individuals walking along. Somewhere (usually behind them) the hail rings out: 'Hey, you there!' One individual (nine times out

18. Hailing as an everyday practice subject to a precise ritual takes a quite 'special' form in the policeman's practice of 'hailing' which concerns the hailing of 'suspects'.

of ten it is the right one) turns round, believing/suspecting/ knowing that it is for him, i.e. recognizing that 'it really is he' who is meant by the hailing. But in reality these things happen without any succession. The existence of ideology and the hailing or interpellation of individuals as subjects are one and the same thing.

I might add: what thus seems to take place outside ideology (to be precise, in the street), in reality takes place in ideology. What really takes place in ideology seems therefore to take place outside it. That is why those who are in ideology believe themselves by definition outside ideology: one of the effects of ideology is the practical *denegation* of the ideological character of ideology by ideology: ideology never says, 'I am ideological'. It is necessary to be outside ideology, i.e. in scientific knowledge, to be able to say: I am in ideology (a quite exceptional case) or (the general case): I was in ideology. As is well known, the accusation of being in ideology only applies to others, never to oneself (unless one is really a Spinozist or a Marxist, which, in this matter, is to be exactly the same thing). Which amounts to saying that ideology *has no outside* (for itself), but at the same time *that it is nothing but outside* (for science and reality).

Spinoza explained this completely two centuries before Marx, who practised it but without explaining it in detail. But let us leave this point, although it is heavy with consequences, consequences which are not just theoretical, but also directly political, since, for example, the whole theory of criticism and self-criticism, the golden rule of the Marxist-Leninist practice of the class struggle, depends on it.

Thus ideology hails or interpellates individuals as subjects. As ideology is eternal, I must now suppress the temporal form in which I have presented the functioning of ideology, and say: ideology has always-already interpellated individuals as subjects, which amounts to making it clear that individuals are always-already interpellated by ideology as subjects, which necessarily leads us to one last proposition: *individuals are always-already subjects.* Hence individuals are 'abstract' with respect to the subjects which they always-already are. This proposition might seem paradoxical.

That an individual is always-already a subject, even before he is born, is nevertheless the plain reality, accessible to everyone and not a paradox at all. Freud shows that individuals are always 'abstract' with respect to the subjects they always-already are, simply by noting the ideological ritual that surrounds the expectation of a 'birth', that 'happy event'. Everyone knows how much and in what way an unborn child is expected. Which amounts to saying, very prosaically, if we agree to drop the 'sentiments', i.e. the forms of family ideology (paternal/maternal/conjugal/fraternal) in which the unborn child is expected: it is certain in advance that it will bear its Father's Name, and will therefore have an identity and be irreplaceable. Before its birth, the child is therefore always-already a subject, appointed as a subject in and by the specific familial ideological configuration in which it is 'expected' once it has been conceived. I hardly need add that this familial ideological configuration is, in its uniqueness, highly structured, and that it is in this implacable and more or less 'pathological' (presupposing that any meaning can be assigned to that term) structure that the former subject-to-be will have to 'find' 'its' place, i.e. 'become' the sexual subject (boy or girl) which it already is in advance. It is clear that this ideological constraint and pre-appointment, and all the rituals of rearing and then education in the family, have some relationship with what Freud studied in the forms of the pre-genital and genital 'stages' of sexuality, i.e. in the 'grip' of what Freud registered by its effects as being the unconscious. But let us leave this point, too, on one side.

Let me go one step further. What I shall now turn my attention to is the way the 'actors' in this *mise en scène* of interpellation, and their respective roles, are reflected in the very structure of all ideology.

An Example: The Christian Religious Ideology

As the formal structure of all ideology is always the same, I shall restrict my analysis to a single example, one accessible to everyone, that of religious ideology, with the proviso that the same demonstration can be produced for ethical, legal, political, aesthetic ideology, etc.

Let us therefore consider the Christian religious ideology. I shall use a rhetorical figure and 'make it speak', i.e. collect into a fictional discourse what it 'says' not only in its two Testaments, its Theologians, Sermons, but also in its practices, its rituals, its ceremonies and its sacraments. The Christian religious ideology says something like this:

It says: I address myself to you, a human individual called Peter (every individual is called by his name, in the passive sense, it is never he who provides his own name), in order to tell you that God exists and that you are answerable to Him. It adds: God addresses himself to you through my voice (Scripture having collected the Word of God, Tradition having transmitted it, Papal Infallibility fixing it for ever on 'nice' points). It says: this is who you are: you are Peter! This is your origin, you were created by God for all eternity, although you were born in the 1920th year of Our Lord! This is your place in the world! This is what you must do! By these means, if you observe the 'law of love' you will be saved, you, Peter, and will become part of the Glorious Body of Christ! Etc. . . .

Now this is quite a familiar and banal discourse, but at the same time quite a surprising one.

Surprising because if we consider that religious ideology is indeed addressed to individuals,[19] in order to 'transform them into subjects', by interpellating the individual, Peter, in order to make him a subject, free to obey or disobey the appeal, i.e. God's commandments; if it calls these individuals by their names, thus recognizing that they are always-already interpellated as subjects with a personal identity (to the extent that Pascal's Christ says: 'It is for you that I have shed this drop of my blood!'); if it interpellates them in such a way that the subject responds: '*Yes, it really is me!*' if it obtains from them the *recognition* that they really do occupy the place it designates for them as theirs in the world, a fixed residence: 'It really is me, I am here, a worker, a boss or a soldier!' in this vale of tears; if it obtains from them the recognition of a destination (eternal life or damnation) according to the respect or contempt they show to 'God's Commandments', Law become Love; – if everything does happen in this way (in the practices of the well-known rituals of baptism, confirmation, communion, confession and extreme unction, etc. . . .), we should note that all this 'procedure' to set up Christian religious subjects is dominated by a strange phenomenon: the fact that there can only be such a multitude of possible religious subjects on the absolute condition that there is a Unique, Absolute, *Other Subject*, i.e. God.

It is convenient to designate this new and remarkable Subject by writing Subject with a capital S to distinguish it from ordinary subjects, with a small s.

It then emerges that the interpellation of individuals as subjects presupposes the 'existence' of a Unique and central Other Subject, in whose Name the religious ideology

19. Although we know that the individual is always already a subject, we go on using this term, convenient because of the contrasting effect it produces.

interpellates all individuals as subjects. All this is clearly[20] written in what is rightly called the Scriptures. 'And it came to pass at that time that God the Lord (Yahweh) spoke to Moses in the cloud. And the Lord cried to Moses, "Moses!" And Moses replied "It is (really) I! I am Moses thy servant, speak and I shall listen!" And the Lord spoke to Moses and said to him, "*I am that I am*" '.

God thus defines himself as the Subject *par excellence*, he who is through himself and for himself ('I am that I am'), and he who interpellates his subject, the individual subjected to him by his very interpellation, i.e. the individual named Moses. And Moses, interpellated-called by his Name, having recognized that it 'really' was he who was called by God, recognizes that he is a subject, a subject *of* God, a subject subjected to God, *a subject through the Subject and subjected to the Subject*. The proof: he obeys him, and makes his people obey God's Commandments.

God is thus the Subject, and Moses and the innumerable subjects of God's people, the Subject's interlocutors-interpellates: his *mirrors*, his *reflections*. Were not men made *in the image* of God? As all theological reflection proves, whereas He 'could' perfectly well have done without men, God needs them, the Subject needs the subjects, just as men need God, the subjects need the Subject. Better: God needs men, the great Subject needs subjects, even in the terrible inversion of his image in them (when the subjects wallow in debauchery, i.e. sin).

Better: God duplicates himself and sends his Son to the Earth, as a mere subject 'forsaken' by him (the long complaint of the Garden of Olives which ends in the Crucifixion), subject but Subject, man but God, to do what prepares the way for the final Redemption, the Resurrection

20. I am quoting in a combined way, not to the letter but 'in spirit and truth'.

of Christ. God thus needs to 'make himself' a man, the Subject needs to become a subject, as if to show empirically, visibly to the eye, tangibly to the hands (see St Thomas) of the subjects, that, if they are subjects, subjected to the Subject, that is solely in order that finally, on Judgement Day, they will re-enter the Lord's Bosom, like Christ, i.e. re-enter the Subject.[21]

Let us decipher into theoretical language this wonderful necessity for the duplication of *the Subject into subjects* and of *the Subject itself into a subject-Subject*.

We observe that the structure of all ideology, interpellating individuals as subjects in the name of a Unique and Absolute Subject is *speculary*, i.e. a mirror-structure, and *doubly* speculary: this mirror duplication is constitutive of ideology and ensures its functioning. Which means that all ideology is *centred*, that the Absolute Subject occupies the unique place of the Centre, and interpellates around it the infinity of individuals into subjects in a double mirror-connexion such that it *subjects* the subjects to the Subject, while giving them in the Subject in which each subject can contemplate its own image (present and future) the *guarantee* that this really concerns them and Him, and that since everything takes place in the Family (the Holy Family: the Family is in essence Holy), 'God will *recognize* his own in it', i.e. those who have recognized God, and have recognized themselves in Him, will be saved.

Let me summarize what we have discovered about ideology in general.

The duplicate mirror-structure of ideology ensures simultaneously:

---

21. The dogma of the Trinity is precisely the theory of the duplication of the Subject (the Father) into a subject (the Son) and of their mirror-connexion (the Holy Spirit).

1. the interpellation of 'individuals' as subjects;

2. their subjection to the Subject;

3. the mutual recognition of subjects and Subject, the subjects' recognition of each other, and finally the subject's recognition of himself;[22]

4. the absolute guarantee that everything really is so, and that on condition that the subjects recognize what they are and behave accordingly, everything will be all right: Amen – '*So be it*'.

Result: caught in this quadruple system of interpellation as subjects, of subjection to the Subject, of universal recognition and of absolute guarantee, the subjects 'work', they 'work by themselves' in the vast majority of cases, with the exception of the 'bad subjects' who on occasion provoke the intervention of one of the detachments of the (repressive) State apparatus. But the vast majority of (good) subjects work all right 'all by themselves', i.e. by ideology (whose concrete forms are realized in the Ideological State Apparatuses). They are inserted into practices governed by the rituals of the ISAs. They 'recognize' the existing state of affairs (*das Bestehende*), that 'it really is true that it is so and not otherwise', and that they must be obedient to God, to their conscience, to the priest, to de Gaulle, to the boss, to the engineer, that thou shalt 'love thy neighbour as thyself', etc. Their concrete, material behaviour is simply the inscription in life of the admirable words of the prayer: '*Amen – So be it*'.

Yes, the subjects 'work by themselves'. The whole

22. Hegel is (unknowingly) an admirable 'theoretician' of ideology insofar as he is a 'theoretician' of Universal Recognition who unfortunately ends up in the ideology of Absolute Knowledge. Feuerbach is an astonishing 'theoretician' of the mirror connexion, who unfortunately ends up in the ideology of the Human Essence. To find the material with which to construct a theory of the guarantee, we must turn to Spinoza.

mystery of this effect lies in the first two moments of the quadruple system I have just discussed, or, if you prefer, in the ambiguity of the term *subject*. In the ordinary use of the term, subject in fact means: (1) a free subjectivity, a centre of initiatives, author of and responsible for its actions; (2) a subjected being, who submits to a higher authority, and is therefore stripped of all freedom except that of freely accepting his submission. This last note gives us the meaning of this ambiguity, which is merely a reflection of the effect which produces it: the individual *is interpellated as a (free) subject in order that he shall submit freely to the commandments of the Subject, i.e. in order that he shall (freely) accept his subjection*, i.e. in order that he shall make the gestures and actions of his subjection 'all by himself'. *There are no subjects except by and for their subjection*. That is why they 'work all by themselves'.

'*So be it!* . . .' This phrase which registers the effect to be obtained proves that it is not 'naturally' so ('naturally': outside the prayer, i.e. outside the ideological intervention). This phrase proves that it *has* to be so if things are to be what they must be, and let us let the words slip: if the reproduction of the relations of production is to be assured, even in the processes of production and circulation, every day, in the 'consciousness', i.e. in the attitudes of the individual-subjects occupying the posts which the socio-technical division of labour assigns to them in production, exploitation, repression, ideologization, scientific practice, etc. Indeed, what is really in question in this mechanism of the mirror recognition of the Subject and of the individuals interpellated as subjects, and of the guarantee given by the Subject to the subjects if they freely accept their subjection to the Subject's 'commandments'? The reality in question in this mechanism, the reality which is necessarily *ignored* (*méconnue*) in the very forms of recognition (ideology = misrecognition/ignorance) is indeed, in the last resort, the reproduction of the relations of production and of the relations deriving from them.

January–April 1969

P.S. If these few schematic theses allow me to illuminate certain aspects of the functioning of the Superstructure and its mode of intervention in the Infrastructure, they are obviously *abstract* and necessarily leave several important problems unanswered, which should be mentioned:

1. The problem of the *total process* of the realization of the reproduction of the relations of production.

As an element of this process, the ISAs *contribute* to this reproduction. But the point of view of their contribution alone is still an abstract one.

It is only within the processes of production and circulation that this reproduction is *realized*. It is realized by the mechanisms of those processes, in which the training of the workers is 'completed', their posts assigned them, etc. It is in the internal mechanisms of these processes that the effect of the different ideologies is felt (above all the effect of legal-ethical ideology).

But this point of view is still an abstract one. For in a class society the relations of production are relations of exploitation, and therefore relations between antagonistic classes. The reproduction of the relations of production, the ultimate aim of the ruling class, cannot therefore be a merely technical operation training and distributing individuals for the different posts in the 'technical division' of labour. In fact there is no 'technical division' of labour except in the ideology of the ruling class: every 'technical' division, every 'technical' organization of labour is the form and mask of a *social* (= class) division and organization of labour. The reproduction of the relations of production can therefore only be a class undertaking. It is realized through a class struggle which counterposes the ruling class and the exploited class.

The *total process* of the realization of the reproduction of the relations of production is therefore still abstract, insofar as it has not adopted the point of view of this class struggle. To adopt the point of view of reproduction is therefore, in the last instance, to adopt the point of view of the class struggle.

2. The problem of the class nature of the ideolog*ies* existing in a social formation.

The 'mechanism' of ideology *in general* is one thing. We have seen that it can be reduced to a few principles expressed in a few words (as 'poor' as those which, according to Marx, define production *in general*, or in Freud, define *the* unconscious *in general*). If there is any truth in it, this mechanism must be *abstract* with respect to every real ideological formation.

I have suggested that the ideologies were *realized* in institutions, in their rituals and their practices, in the ISAs. We have seen that on this basis they contribute to that form of class struggle, vital for the ruling class, the reproduction of the relations of production. But the point of view itself, however real, is still an abstract one.

In fact, the State and its Apparatuses only have meaning from the point of view of the class struggle, as an apparatus of class struggle ensuring class oppression and guaranteeing the conditions of exploitation and its reproduction. But there is no class struggle without antagonistic classes. Whoever says class struggle of the ruling class says resistance, revolt and class struggle of the ruled class.

That is why the ISAs are not the realization of ideology *in general*, nor even the conflict-free realization of the ideology of the ruling class. The ideology of the ruling class does not become the ruling ideology by the grace of God, nor even by virtue of the seizure of State power alone. It is by the installation of the ISAs in which this ideology is realized and realizes itself that it becomes the ruling ideology. But this installation is not achieved all by itself; on the contrary, it is the stake in a very bitter and continuous class struggle: first against the former ruling classes and their positions in the old and new ISAs, then against the exploited class.

But this point of view of the class struggle in the ISAs is still an abstract one. In fact, the class struggle in the ISAs is indeed an aspect of the class struggle, sometimes an important and symptomatic one: e.g. the anti-religious struggle in the eighteenth century, or the 'crisis' of the educational ISA in every capitalist country today. But the class struggles in the ISAs is only one aspect of a class struggle which goes beyond the ISAs. The ideology that a class in power makes the ruling ideology in its ISAs is indeed 'realized' in those ISAs, but it goes beyond them, for it comes from elsewhere. Similarly, the ideology that a ruled class manages to defend in and against such ISAs goes beyond them, for it comes from elsewhere.

It is only from the point of view of the classes, i.e. of the class struggle, that it is possible to explain the ideolog*ies* existing in a social formation. Not only is it from this starting-point that it is possible to explain the realization of the ruling ideology in the ISAs and of the forms of class struggle for which the ISAs are the seat and the stake. But it is also and above all from this starting-point that it is possible to understand the provenance of the ideologies which are realized in the ISAs and confront one another there. For if it is true that the ISAs represent the *form* in which the ideology of the ruling class must *necessarily* be realized, and the form in which the ideology of the ruled class must *necessarily* be measured and confronted, ideologies are not 'born' in the ISAs but from the social classes at grips in the class struggle: from their conditions of existence, their practices, their experience of the struggle, etc.

April 1970

Appendix

PUBLISHER'S NOTE TO 'FREUD AND LACAN'

Louis Althusser agreed to let New Left Review *reproduce the following article, which was written in 1964 and published in the French Communist Party journal,* La Nouvelle Critique.

In a letter to the translator (21 February 1969), Louis Althusser wrote: 'There is a danger that this text will be misunderstood, unless it is taken for what it then objectively was: a philosophical intervention *urging members of the* PCF *to recognize the* scientificity *of psycho-analysis, of Freud's work, and the importance of Lacan's interpretation of it. Hence it was polemical, for psycho-analysis had been* officially *condemned in the fifties as "a reactionary ideology", and, despite some modification, this condemnation still dominated the situation when I wrote this article. This exceptional situation must be taken into account when the meaning of my interpretation is assessed today.'*

Louis Althusser also warned English readers that his article contained theses that must 'either *be corrected, or* expanded'.

'In particular, in the article Lacan's theory is presented in terms which, despite all precautions, have "culturalist" overtones (whereas Lacan's theory is profoundly anti-*culturalist).*

'On the other hand, the suggestions at the end of the article are correct and deserve a much extended treatment, that is, the

discussion of the forms of familial ideology, *and of the crucial role they play in initiating the functioning of the instance that Freud called "the unconscious", but which should be re-christened as soon as a better term is found.*

'*This mention of the forms of familial ideology (the ideology of paternity-maternity-conjugality-infancy and their inter-actions) is crucial, for it implies the following conclusion – that Lacan could not express, given his theoretical formation – that is, that* no theory of psycho-analysis can be produced without basing it on historical materialism (*on which the theory of the formations of familial ideology depends, in the last instance*).'

AUTHOR'S PREFATORY NOTE

Let us admit, without prevarication: anyone today who merely wants to understand Freud's revolutionary dis-covery, who wants to know what it means as well as just recognizing its existence, has to make a great theoretical and critical effort in order to cross the vast space of ideological prejudice that divides us from Freud. For not only has Freud's discovery been reduced, as we shall see, to disciplines which are essentially foreign to it (biology, psychology, sociology, philosophy); not only have many psycho-analysts (notably in the American school) becomes accomplices to this revisionism; but, more important, this revisionism has itself objectively assisted the fantastic ideological exploita-tion whose object and victim psycho-analysis has been. Not without good reason did French Marxists once (in 1948) denounce this exploitation as a 'reactionary ideology' which furnished arguments for the ideological struggle against Marxism, and a practical instrument for the intimi-dation and mystification of consciousnesses.

But today it must also be said that, in their own way, these same Marxists were directly or indirectly the first victims of the ideology they denounced; for they confused this ideology and Freud's revolutionary discovery, thereby adopting in practice the enemy's position, accepting his conditions and recognizing the image he had imposed on them as the supposed reality of psycho-analysis. The whole history of the relations between Marxism and psycho-analysis depends essentially on this confusion, this imposture.

That this was particularly difficult to avoid we can understand from the function of this ideology: the 'dominant' ideas, in this case, were playing their 'dominating' role to perfection, ruling unrecognized over the very minds that were trying to fight them. But it is explained by the existence of the pyscho-analytic revisionism that made this exploitation possible: the fall into ideology began in fact with the fall of psycho-analysis into biologism, psychologism and sociologism.

We can also see that this revisionism could derive its authority from the ambiguity of some of Freud's concepts, for, like all inventors, Freud was forced to think his discovery in existing theoretical concepts, i.e. concepts designed for other purposes (was not Marx, too, forced to think his discovery in certain Hegelian concepts?). This will come as no surprise to anyone at all familiar with the history of new sciences – and at all careful to discern the irreducible element of a discovery and of its objects in the concepts in which it was expressed at its birth, but which, out-dated by the advance of knowledge, may later mask it.

So a return to Freud today demands:

1. Not only that we reject the ideological layers of the reactionary exploitation of Freud as a crude mystification;

2. but also that we avoid the more subtle ambiguities of

psycho-analytic revisionism, sustained as they are by the prestige of certain more or less scientific disciplines;

3. and finally that we commit ourselves to a serious effort of historico-theoretical criticism in order to identify and define, in the concepts Freud had to use, the true *epistemological relation* between these concepts and their thought content.

Without this triple labour of ideological criticism (1,2) and epistemological elucidation (3), which, in France, has been initiated in practice by Lacan, Freud's discovery in its specificity will remain beyond our reach. And, more serious, we will take as Freud precisely what has been put within our reach, precisely what we aimed to reject (the reactionary ideological exploitation of Freud), or subscribed to more or less thoughtlessly (the different forms of bio-psycho-sociological revisionism). In either case, we would remain prisoners, at different levels, of the explicit or implicit categories of ideological exploitation and theoretical revisionism. Marxists, who know from their own experience the deformations Marx's enemies have imposed on his thought, can see why Freud could suffer the same fate, in his own way, and why an authentic 'return to Freud' is of such theoretical importance.

They will concede that if such a short article proposes to introduce a problem of this importance without betraying it, it must confine itself to the essential, it must situate the *object* of psycho-analysis so as to give a first definition of it, in concepts that allow its *location*, the indispensable precondition for its elucidation. They will concede therefore that, as far as possible, these concepts should be introduced in a rigorous form, as in any scientific discipline; to vulgarize them in an over-approximate commentary would banalize them, while an analysis that really drew them out would require much more space.

An accurate assessment of these concepts can only come from the serious study of Freud and Lacan which each one of us can undertake; the same is true for the definition of the still unsolved problems of this theoretical discipline already rich in results and promises.

Freud and Lacan

Friends have correctly criticized me for discussing Lacan in three lines.[1] This was too much for what I was saying about him, and too little for the conclusions that I drew from him. They have asked me for a few words to justify both the allusion and its object. Here they are – a few words, where a book is needed.

In the history of Western Reason, every care, foresight, precaution and warning has been devoted to births. Pre-natal therapy is institutional. When a young science is born, the family circle is always ready for astonishment, jubilation and baptism. For a long time, every child, even the found-ling, has been reputed the son of a father, and when it is a prodigy, the fathers would fight at the gate if it were not for the mother and the respect due to her. In our crowded world, a place is allocated for birth, a place is even allocated for the prediction of a birth: 'prospective'.

1. *Revue de l'Enseignement philosophique*, June-July 1963, 'Philosophie et sciences humaines', p. 7 and p. 11, n.14: 'Marx based his theory on the rejection of the myth of the "*homo œconomicus*", Freud based his theory on the rejection of the myth of the "*homo psychologicus*". Lacan has seen and understood Freud's liberating rupture. He has understood it in the fullest sense of the term, taking it rigorously at its word and forcing it to produce its own consequences, without concessions or quarter. It may be that, like everyone else, he errs in the detail or even the choice of his philosophical bearings; but we owe him the *essential*.'

To my knowledge, the nineteenth century saw the birth of two or three children that were not expected: Marx, Nietzsche and Freud. 'Natural' children, in the sense that nature offends customs, principles, morality and good breeding: nature is the rule violated, the unmarried mother, hence the absence of a legal father. Western Reason makes a fatherless child pay heavily. Marx, Nietzsche and Freud had to foot the often terrible bill of survival: a price compounded of exclusion, condemnation, insult, poverty, hunger and death, or madness. I speak only of them (other unfortunates might be mentioned who lived their death sentences in colour, sound and poetry). I speak only of them because they were the births of sciences or of criticism.

That Freud knew poverty, calumny and persecution, that his spirit was well enough anchored to withstand, and interpret, all the insults of the age – these things may have something to do with certain of the limits and dead-ends of his genius. An examination of this point is probably premature. Let us instead consider Freud's solitude in his own times. I do not mean human solitude (he had teachers and friends, though he went hungry), I mean *theoretical* solitude. For when he wanted to think i.e. to express in the form of a rigorous system of abstract concepts the extraordinary discovery that met him every day in his *practice*, search as he might for theoretical precedents, fathers in theory, he could find none. He had to cope with the following situation: to be himself his own father, to construct with his own craftsman's hands the theoretical space in which to situate his discovery, to weave with thread borrowed intuitively left and right the great net with which to catch in the depths of blind experience the teeming fish of the unconscious, which men call dumb because it speaks even while they sleep.

To express this in Kantian terms: Freud had to think his

discovery and his practice in *imported* concepts, concepts borrowed from the thermodynamic physics then dominant, from the political economy and biology of his time. With no legal inheritance behind him – except for a parcel of philosophical concepts (consciousness, preconsciousness, unconsciousness, etc.) which were probably more of a hindrance than a help as they were marked by a problematic of consciousness present even in its reservations – without any ancestral endowment whatever, his only forerunners writers – Sophocles, Shakespeare, Molière, Goethe – or proverbs, etc. Theoretically, Freud set up in business alone: producing his own 'home-made' concepts under the protection of imported concepts borrowed from the sciences as they existed, and, it should be said, from within the horizons of the ideological world in which these concepts swam.

That is how Freud comes to us. A long series of profound texts, sometimes clear, sometimes obscure, often enigmatic and contradictory, problematic, and armed with concepts many of which seem to us at first sight to be out of date, inadequate for their content, or surpassed. For today we cannot doubt the existence of this content: analytic practice itself, its effect.

So let us summarize the object Freud is for us:

1. A practice (the analytic cure). 2. A technique (the method of the cure) that gives rise to an abstract exposition with the appearance of a theory. 3. A theory which has a relation with the practice and the technique. This organic practical (1), technical (2) and theoretical (3) whole recalls the structure of every scientific discipline. *Formally*, what Freud gives us does have the structure of a science. Formally; for the difficulties of Freud's conceptual terminology, the sometimes material disproportion between his concepts and their content, suggest the question: in this organic

practico-technico-theoretical whole do we have a whole that is truly stabilized and founded at the scientific level? In other words, is the theory really theory in the scientific sense? Or is it not, on the contrary, a simple transposition into theory of the methodology of the practice (the cure)? Hence the very common modern view that beneath its theoretical exterior (which we owe to worthy but vain pretensions of Freud himself), psycho-analysis remains a mere practice that does sometimes give results, but not always; a mere practice extended into a technique (rules of analytic method), but *without a theory*, at least without a true theory: what it calls theory being merely the blind technical concepts in which it reflects the rules of its practice; a mere practice without theory . . . perhaps then, even simply a kind of magic? that succeeds, like all magic, because of its prestige – and its prestige, applied to the fulfilment of a social need or demand, therefore its only justification, its real justification. Lévi-Strauss would then have theorized this *magic*, this *social* practice, psycho-analysis, by pointing out the *shaman* as the ancestor of Freud.

A practice pregnant with a half-silent theory? A practice proud or ashamed to be merely the social magic of modern times? What then is psychoanalysis?

I

Lacan's first word is to say: in principle, Freud founded a *science*. A new science which was the science of a new object: the unconscious.

A rigorous statement. If psycho-analysis is a science because it is the science of a distinct object, it is also a science with the structure of all sciences: it has a *theory* and a *technique* (method) that make possible the knowledge and transformation of its object in a specific *practice*. As in every authentically constituted science, the practice is not the absolute of the science but a theoretically subordinate moment; the moment in which the theory, having become method (technique), comes into theoretical contact (knowledge) or practical contact (cure) with its specific object (the unconscious).

If this thesis is correct, analytical practice (the cure), which absorbs all the attention of those interpreters and philosophers eager for the intimacy of the confidential couple in which avowed sickness and professional medical secrecy exchange the sacred promises of intersubjectivity, does not contain the secrets of psycho-analysis; it only contains one part of the reality of psycho-analysis, the part which exists in the practice. It does not contain its theoretical secrets. If this thesis is correct, neither do the technique and method contain the secrets of psycho-analysis, except as every method does, by delegation, not from the practice but from the theory. Only the theory contains them, as in every scientific discipline.

In a hundred places in his work, Freud calls himself a theoretician; he compares psycho-analysis, as far as its scientificity is concerned, with the physical sciences that stem from Galileo, he repeats that the practice (cure) and analytical technique (analytical method) are only authentic because they are based on a scientific *theory*. Freud says time and again that a practice and a technique, even if they give results, do not deserve the name of science unless a theory gives them the right to it, not by mere declaration, but by rigorous proof.

Lacan's first word is to take these words literally. And to draw the conclusion: a return to Freud to seek out, distinguish and pin-point in him the theory from which all the rest, both practical and technical, stems by right.

A return to Freud. Why this new return to the source?

Lacan does not return to Freud as Husserl does to Galileo or Thales, to capture a birth at its birth – i.e. to achieve that religious philosophical preconception, purity, which like all water bubbling up out of the ground, is only pure at the very instant, the pure instant of its birth, in the pure passage from non-science to science. For Lacan, this passage is not pure, it is still impure: purity comes after the still 'muddy' passage (the invisible mud of its past suspended in the new-born water which pretends transparency, i.e. innocence). A return to Freud means: a return to the theory established, fixed and founded firmly in Freud himself, to the mature, reflected, supported and verified theory, to the advanced theory that has settled down in life (including practical life) to build its home, produce its method and give birth to its practice. The return to Freud is not a return to Freud's birth: but a return to his *maturity*. Freud's youth, the moving passage from not-yet-science to science (the period of the relations with Charcot, Bernheim, Breuer, up to the *Studies in Hysteria* – 1895) may indeed be of interest to us, but on a quite different level: as an example of the archaeology of a science – or as a negative index of immaturity, thereby precisely dating maturity and its arrival. The youth of a science is its prime of life; before this age it is old, its age the age of the preconceptions by which it lives, as a child does the preconceptions and hence the age of its parents.

That a young, and hence mature theory can relapse into childhood, i.e. into the preconceptions of its elders and their descendants, is proved by the whole history of psycho-analysis. This is the deeper meaning of the return to Freud proclaimed by Lacan. We must return to Freud to return to the maturity of Freudian theory, not to its childhood, but to its prime, which is its true youth – we must return to Freud beyond the theoretical childishness, the relapse into childhood in which all or a part of contemporary psycho-analysis, particularly in America, savours the advantages of surrender.

This relapse into childhood has a name that pheno-menologists will understand straight away: psychologism – or another that Marxists will understand straight away: pragmatism. The modern history of psycho-analysis illustrates Lacan's judgement. Western Reason (legal, religious, moral and political *as well as* scientific) will only agree to conclude a pact of peaceful coexistence with psycho-analysis after years of non-recognition, contempt and insults – means that are still available anyway if all else fails – on condition of annexing it to its own sciences or myths: to psychology, whether behaviourist (Dalbiez), phenomenological (Mer-leau-Ponty) or existentialist (Sartre); to a more or less Jacksonian bio-neurology (Ey); to 'sociology' of the 'cul-turalist' or 'anthropological' type (dominant in the USA: Kardiner, Margaret Mead, etc); and to philosophy (cf. Sartre's 'existentialist psychoanalysis', Binswanger's *'Das-einanalyse'*, etc.). To these confusions, to this mytholo-gization of psycho-analysis, a discipline officially recognized at the price of compromise alliances sealed with *imaginary* ties of adoption but very real powers, some psycho-analysts have subscribed, only too happy to emerge at last from their theoretical ghetto, to be 'recognized' as full members of the great family of psychology, neurology, psychiatry, medicine, sociology, anthropology, philosophy – only too happy to certify their practical success with this 'theoretical' recog-nition which at last, after decades of insults and exile, confers on them citizen's rights in the world: the world of science, medicine and philosophy. They were not alerted to the suspicious side of this agreement, believing that the world was coming round to their positions – when they were themselves, with these honours, coming round to the world's positions – preferring its honours to its insults.

They thereby forgot that a science is only a science if it can claim a right to an object *of its own* – an object that is its own and its own *only* – not a mere foothold in an object loaned, conceded or abandoned by another science, one of the latter's 'aspects', the *leavings* that can be rehashed in the kitchen once the master of the house has eaten his fill. Concretely, if the whole of psycho-analysis is reduced to behaviourist or Pavlovian 'conditioning' in early childhood; if it is reduced to a dialectic of the *stages* which Freud's terminology designates as oral, anal and genital, latency and puberty; if, finally, it is reduced to the primitive experience of the Hegelian struggle, of the phenomenological for-others, or of the Heideggerian 'gulf' of being; if all psycho-analysis is merely this art of assimilating the leavings of neurology, biology, psychology, anthropology and philosophy, what can it claim as its specific object, what really distinguishes it from these disciplines and makes it in the full sense a science?[2]

2. The most dangerous of these temptations are those of *philosophy* (which gladly reduces the whole of the psycho-analysis to the dual experience of the cure and thereby 'verifies' the themes of phenomenological intersubjectivity, of the existence-project, or more generally of personalism); of *psychology* which appropriates most of the categories of psycho-analysis as so many attributes of a 'subject' in which, manifestly, it sees no problem; finally, of sociology which comes to the aid of psychology by providing it with an objective content for the 'reality principle' (social and familial imperatives) which the 'subject' need only 'internalize' to be armed with a 'super-ego' and the corresponding categories. Thus subordinated to psychology or sociology psycho-analysis is usually reduced to a technique of 'emotional' or 'affective' re-adaptation, or to a re-education of the 'relational function', neither of which have anything to do with its real object – but which unfortunately respond to a major demand, and what is more, to a demand that is highly tendentious in the contemporary world. Through this bias, psycho-analysis has become an article of mass consumption in modern culture, i.e. in modern ideology.

It is here that Lacan intervenes: he defends the irreducibility of analysis against these 'reductions' and deviations, which dominate most contemporary theoretical interpretations; he defends its irreducibility, which means *the irreducibility of its object*. That this defence requires an uncommon lucidity and firmness, sufficient to repulse all the voraciously hospitable assaults of the disciplines I have listed, cannot be doubted by anyone who has ever in his life measured the need for security (theoretical, moral, social and economic), i.e. the uneasiness, of corporations (whose status is indissolubly scientific-professional-legal-economic) whose balance and comfort is threatened by the appearance of a unique discipline that forces them all to re-investigate not only their own disciplines but the reasons why they believe in them, i.e. to doubt them, by the appearance of a science which, however little it is believed, threatens to violate the existing frontiers and hence to alter the *status quo* of several disciplines. Hence the contained passion and passionate contention of Lacan's language, unable to live or survive except in a state of alert and accusation: the language of a man of the besieged vanguard, condemned by the crushing strength of the threatened structures and corporations to forestall their blows, or at least to feint a response to them before they are delivered, thus discouraging the opponents from crushing him beneath their assault. Hence also the often paradoxical resort to the security provided by philosophies completely foreign to his scientific undertaking (Hegel, Heidegger), as so many intimidating witnesses thrown in the faces of part of his audience to retain their respect; and as so many witnesses to a possible objectivity, the natural ally of his thought, to reassure or educate the rest. As this resort was almost indispensable to sustain a discourse addressed *from within* to the medical profession alone, one would have to ignore both the conceptual weakness of medical studies in general and the profound need for theory felt by the best medical men, to condemn it out of hand. And since I am dealing with his language, the language which is the sum total of his prestige for some of the audience ('the Góngora of psycho-analysis', 'the Grand Dragon', the great officiant of an esoteric cult in which gesture, hushedness and solemnity can constitute the ritual of a real communication – or of a quite 'Parisian' fascination) – and for the rest (above all scientists or philosophers) his 'artifice', his strangeness and his 'hermeticism', it is clear that it bears some relation to the conditions of his practice as a teacher: since he has to teach the theory of the unconscious to doctors, analysts or analy-sands, in the rhetoric of his speech Lacan provides them with a dumbshow equivalent of the language of the un-conscious (which, as is well known, is in its ultimate essence *'Witz'*, successful or unsuccessful pun and metaphor): the equivalent of the lived experience of their practice, whether as analyst or as analysand.

An understanding of this language's ideological and educational preconditions – i.e. the ability to maintain the distance of historical and theoretical 'exteriority' from its pedagogic 'interiority' – is enough to let us discern its objective meaning and scope – and recognize its basic proposal: to give Freud's discovery its measure in theo-retical concepts by defining as rigorously as is possible today the *unconscious* and its 'laws', its whole object.

2

What is the *object* of psycho-analysis? It is *what* analytical technique deals with in the analytical practice of the cure, i.e. not the cure itself, not that supposedly dual system which is tailor-made for any phenomenology or morality –

but the '*effects*', prolonged into the surviving adult, of the extraordinary adventure which from birth to the liquidation of the Oedipal phase transforms a small animal conceived by a man and a woman into a small human child.

One of the 'effects' of the humanization of the small biological creature that results from human parturition: there in its place is the object of psycho-analysis, an object which has a simple name: '*the unconscious*'.

That this small biological being survives, and not as a 'wolf-child', that has become a little wolf or bear (as displayed in the princely courts of the eighteenth century), but as a *human child* (having escaped all childhood deaths, many of which are human deaths, deaths punishing the failure of humanization), that is the test all adult men have passed: they are the *never forgetful* witnesses, and very often the victims, of this victory, bearing in their most hidden, i.e. in their most clamorous parts, the wounds, weaknesses and stiffnesses that result from this struggle for human life or death. Some, the majority, have emerged more or less unscathed – or at least, give this out to be the case; many of these veretans bear the marks throughout their lives; some will die from their fight, though at some remove, the old wounds suddenly opening again in psychotic explosion, in madness, the ultimate compulsion of a 'negative therapeutic reaction'; others, more numerous, as 'normally' as you like, in the guise of an 'organic' decay. Humanity only inscribes its official deaths on its war memorials: those who were able to die on time, i.e. late, as men, in human wars in which only *human* wolves and gods tear and sacrifice one another. In its sole survivors, psycho-analysis is concerned with another struggle, with the only war without memoirs or memorials, the war humanity pretends it has never declared, the war it always thinks it has won in advance, simply because humanity is nothing but surviving this war, living and bearing children as culture in human culture: a war which is continually declared in each of its sons, who, projected, deformed and rejected, are required, each by himself in solitude and against death, to take the long forced march which makes mammiferous larvae into human children, *masculine* or *feminine subjects*.

This object is no business of the biologist's: this story is certainly not biological! – since from the beginning it is completely dominated by the constraint of the sexed human order that each mother engraves on the small human animal in maternal 'love' or hatred, starting from its alimentary rhythm and training. History, 'sociology' or anthropology have no business here, and this is no surprise for they deal with society and therefore with culture, i.e. with what is no longer this small animal – which only becomes human-sexual by crossing the infinite divide that separates life from humanity, the biological from the historical, 'nature' from 'culture'. Psychology is lost here, and this is hardly strange for it thinks that in its 'object' it is dealing with some *human* 'nature' or 'non-nature', with the genesis of this existent, identified and certified by culture itself (by the human) – when the object of psycho-analysis is the question with absolute priority, whether to be born or not to be (*naître ou n'être pas*), the aleatory abyss of the human-sexual itself in every human scion. Here 'philosophy' loses its bearings and its cover (*'repères'* and *'repaires'*), naturally! – for these unique origins rob it of the only origins it renders homage to for its existence: God, reason, consciousness, history and culture. It is clear that the object of psycho-analysis may be specific and that the modality of its material as well as the specificity of its 'mechanisms' (to use one of Freud's terms) are of quite another kind than the material and 'mechanisms' which are known to the biologist, the neurologist, the anthropologist, the sociologist, the psychologist and the philosopher. We need only recognize this specificity and hence the distinctness of the object that it derives from, in order to recognize the radical right of psycho-analysis to a specificity of its concepts in line with the specifiicity of its object: the unconcious and its effects.

3

Lacan would be the first to admit that his attempted theorization would have been impossible were it not for the emergence of a new science: *linguistics*. It is in the nature of the history of the sciences that one science may often not become a science except by recourse to a detour through other sciences, not only sciences that existed at its baptism but also some new late-comer among sciences that needed time before it could be born. The temporary opacity of the shadow cast on Freudian theory by the model of Helmholtz and Maxwell's thermodynamic physics has been dispersed today by the light that structural linguistics throws on it object, making possible an intelligible approach to that object. Freud himself said that everything depended on language. Lacan makes this more precise: 'the discourse of the unconscious is structured like a language'. In his first great work *The Interpretation of Dreams* (which is not anecdotal and superficial as is frequently suggested, but fundamental), Freud studied the 'mechanisms' and 'laws' of dreams, reducing their variants to two: *displacement* and *condensation*. Lacan recognized these as two essential figures of speech, called in linguistics metonymy and metaphor. Hence slips, failures, jokes and symptoms, like the elements of dreams themselves, became *signifiers*, inscribed in the chain of an unconscious discourse, doubling silently, i.e. deafeningly, in the misrecognition of 'repression', the chain of the human subject's verbal discourse. Hence we were introduced to the paradox, formally familiar to linguistics, of a double yet single discourse, unconscious yet verbal, having for its double field only a single field, with no beyond except in itself: the field of the 'Signifying Chain'. Hence the most important acquisitions of de Saussure and of the linguistics that descends from him began to play a justified part in the understanding of the process of the unconscious as well as that of the verbal discourse of the subject and of their inter-relationship, i.e. of their identical relation and non-relation in other words, of their reduplication and dislocation (*décalage*). Thereby philosophico-idealist interpretations of the unconscious as a second consciousness, of the unconscious as bad faith (Sartre), of the unconscious as the cankerous survival of a non-current structure or non-sense (Merleau-Ponty), all the interpretations of the unconscious as a biologico-archetypical 'id' (Jung) became what they were: not the beginnings of a theory but null 'theories', ideological misunderstandings.

It remained to define (I am forced into the crudest schematism, but how could I avoid it in such a short article?) the meaning of this *primacy* of the formal structure of language and its 'mechanisms' as they are encountered in the practice of analytical interpretation, as a function of the very foundations of this practice: its object, i.e. the 'effects' still present in the survivors of the forced 'humanization' of the small human animal into a *man* or a *woman*. This question cannot be answered merely by invoking the factual primacy of language as the sole object and means of analytical practice. Everything that happens in the cure does take place in and through language (including silence, its rhythms and scansions). But it is necessary to show *why* and *how* in principle the factual role of language in the cure as both raw material of analytic practice and means of production of its effects (the passage, as Lacan puts it, from an 'empty speech' to a 'full speech'), is only founded in fact in analytical practice because it is founded in *principle* in its object, the object that, in the last analysis, founds this practice and its technique: hence, since it is a science, in the *theory* of its object.

Herein no doubt lies the most original aspect of Lacan's work, his discovery. Lacan has shown that this transition from (ultimately purely) biological existence to human existence (the human child) is achieved within the Law of Order, the law I shall call the Law of Culture, and that this Law of Order is confounded in its *formal* essence with the order of language. What are we to understand by this formula, at first sight so enigmatic? Firstly, that the *whole of this transition* can only be grasped in terms of a recurrent language, as designated by the language of the adult or child in a *cure situation*, designated, assigned and localized within the law of language in which is established and pre-sented all human order, i.e. every human role. Secondly, that in this assignment by the language of the cure appears the current, constant presence of the absolute effectiveness of order in the transition itself, of the Law of Culture in humanization.

To give some idea of this in a very few words, I shall indicate the two great moments of this *transition*. 1. The moment of the dual pre-Oedipal intercourse, in which the child, concerned with nothing but one alter-ego, the mother, who punctuates its life by her presence (*da!*) and absence (*fort!*),[3] lives this dual intercourse in the mode of the imaginary fascination of the ego, being itself *that* other, *any*

3. These are the two German expressions made famous by Freud, with which a small child under his observation sanctioned the appearance and disap-pearance of its mother by the manipulation of an arbitrary object that 'represented' her: a cotton-reel.

other, *every* other, all *the others* of primary narcissistic identification, never able to take up the objectifying distance of the third *vis-à-vis* either the other or itself; 2. the Oedipal moment, in which a ternary structure emerges against the background of the dual structure, when the third (the father) intrudes on the imaginary satisfaction of dual fascination, overthrows its economy, destroys its fascinations, and introduces the child to what Lacan calls the Symbolic Order, the order of objectifying language that will finally allow him to say: I, you, he, she or it, that will therefore allow the small child to situate itself as a *human child* in a world of adult thirds.

Hence two great moments: 1. that of the imaginary (pre-Oedipal); 2. that of the symbolic (Oedipal resolution), or, to use a different language, that of objectivity recognized in its (symbolic) use, but not yet known (the knowledge of objectivity arising at a quite different 'age' and also from a quite different practice).

And the crucial point that Lacan has illuminated is this: these two moments are dominated, governed and marked by a single Law, the *Law of the Symbolic*. Even the moment of the imaginary, which, for clarity's sake, I have just presented as *preceding* the symbolic, as distinct from it – hence as the first moment in which the child *lives* its immediate intercourse with a human being (its mother) without recognizing it practically as the symbolic intercourse it is (i.e. as the intercourse of a small human child with a human mother) – *is marked and structured in its dialectic by the dialectic of the Symbolic Order itself*, i.e. by the dialectic of human Order, of the human norm (the norms of the temporal rhythms of feeding, hygiene, behaviour, of the concrete attitudes of recognition – the child's acceptance, rejection, yes and no being merely the small change, the *empirical* modalities of this constitutive Order,

the Order of Law and of the Right of attributory or exclus-
ory assignment), in the form of the Order of the signifier
itself, i.e., in the form of an Order *formally* identical with
the order of language.[4]

Where a superficial or prejudiced reading of Freud has
only seen happy, lawless childhood, the paradise of 'poly-
morphous perversity', a kind of state of nature only punct-
uated by stages of a biological type linked with the func-
tional primacy of some part of the human body, the site of a
'vital' need (oral, anal, genital),[5] Lacan demonstrates the
effectiveness of the Order, the Law, that has been lying in
wait for each infant born since before his birth, and seizes
him before his first cry, assigning to him his place and role,
and hence his fixed destination. Each stage traversed by the
sexed infant is traversed in the realm of Law, of the codes of
human assignment, communication and non-communica-
tion; his 'satisfactions' bear the indelible and constitutive
mark of the Law, of the claims of human Law, that, like all

4. *Formally*: for the Law of Culture, which is first introduced as language
and whose first form is language, is not exhausted by language; its content is
the real kinship structures and the determinate ideological formations in
which the persons inscribed in these structures live their functions. It is not
enough to know that the Western family is patriarchal and exogamic (kinship
structures) – we must also work out the ideological formations that govern
paternity, maternity, conjugality and childhood: what are 'husband-and-
wife-being', 'father-being', 'mother-being' and 'child-being' in the modern
world? A mass of research remains to be done on these ideological formations.
This is a task for *historical materialism*.
5. A branch of neuro-biology and one of psychology have been only too
pleased to discover in Freud a theory of 'stages', and they have not hesitated
to translate it directly and exhaustively into a theory of 'stadial growth', either
neuro-biological or bio-neuro-psychological – mechanically assigning to
neuro-biological growth the role of an 'essence' for which the Freudian
'stages' are merely the 'phenomena' pure and simple. This perspective is
nothing but a re-edition of the old theory of mechanical parallelism. This is
directed particularly towards the disciples of Wallon, for Wallon himself did
not take any notice of Freud.

law, cannot be 'ignored' by anyone, least of all by those ignorant of it, but may be evaded or violated by everyone, above all by its most faithful adherents. That is why any reduction of childhood traumas to a balance of 'biological frustrations' alone, is in principle erroneous, since the Law that covers them, as a Law, abstracts from all contents, exists and acts as a Law only in and by this abstraction, and the infant submits to this rule and receives it from his first breath.[6] This is the beginning, and has always been the beginning, even where there is no living father, of the official presence of the Father (who is Law), hence of the Order of the human signifier, i.e. of the Law of Culture: this discourse, the absolute precondition of any discourse, this discourse present at the top, i.e. absent in the depths, in all verbal discourse, the discourse of this Order, this discourse of the Other, of the great Third, which is this Order itself: *the discourse of the unconscious*. This gives us a hold, a *conceptual* hold on the unconscious, which is in each human being the absolute place where his particular discourse seeks its own place, seeks, misses, and in missing, finds its own

---

6. There is a risk that the theoretical scope of this formal condition may be misconstrued, if this is countered by citing the apparently biological concepts (libido, affects, instincts, desire) in which Freud thinks the 'content' of the unconscious. For example, when he says that the dream is a '*wish-fulfilment*' (*Wunscherfüllung*). The sense here is the same as the sense in which Lacan opposes man's 'empty speech' to his 'full speech', as to the language of unconscious 'desire'. But only on the basis of this formal condition do these (apparently biological) concepts obtain their authentic meaning, or can this meaning be assigned and thought and a curative technique defined and applied. Desire, the basic category of the unconscious, is only intelligible in its specificity as the sole meaning of the discourse of the human subject's unconscious: the meaning that emerges in and through the 'play' of the signifying chain which makes up the discourse of the unconscious. As such, 'desire' is marked by the structure that commands human development. As such, desire is radically distinct from organic and essentially biological 'need'. There is no essential continuity between organic need and unconscious

place, its own anchor to its place, in the imposition, imposture, complicity and denegation of its own imaginary fascinations.

That in the Oedipal phase the sexed child becomes a sexual human child (man or woman) by testing its imaginary fantasms against the Symbolic, and if all 'goes well' finally becomes and accepts itself as what it is: a little boy or little girl among adults, with the rights of a child in this adult world, and, like all children, with the full *right* to become one day 'like daddy', i.e. a masculine human being with a wife (and no longer only a mother), or 'like mummy', i.e. a feminine human being with a husband (and not just a father) – these things are only the destination of the long forced march towards human childhood.

That all the material of this ultimate drama is provided by a previously formed language, which, in the Oedipal phase, is centred and arranged wholly around the signifier *phallus*: the emblem of the Father, the emblem of right, of the Law, the fantasy image of all Right – this may seem astonishing or arbitrary, but all psycho-analysts attest to it as a fact of experience.

---

desire, any more than there is between man's biological existence and his historical existence. Desire is determined in its ambiguous being (its 'failure-in-being' – *manque à être* – says Lacan) by the structure of the Order that imposes its mark on it and destines it for a placeless existence, the existence of repression, for its resources as well as for its disappointments. The specific reality of desire cannot be reached by way of organic need any more than the specific reality of historical existence can be reached by way of the biological existence of 'man'. On the contrary: just as it is the categories of history that allow us to define the specificity of man's historical existence, including some apparently purely biological determinations such as his 'needs' or demographic phenomena, by distinguishing his historical existence from a purely biological existence – similarly, it is the essential categories of the unconscious that allow us to grasp and define the very meaning of desire by distinguishing it from the biological realities that support it (exactly as biological existence supports historical existence) but neither *constitute*, nor *determine* it.

The last Oedipal stage, 'castration', shows us why. When the small boy lives and resolves the tragic and beneficial situation of castration, he accepts the fact that he *has not* the same Right (phallus) as his father, in particular, that he has not the same Right as his father over his mother, who is thereby revealed as endowed with the intolerable status of double use, mother for the small boy, wife for the father; but by accepting that he has not the same right as his father, he gains the assurance that one day, *later on*, when he grows up, he will get the right which is now refused him through his lack of 'means'. He has only a little right, which will grow big if he will grow big himself by taking care to 'mind his p's and q's' (*'manger sa soupe'*). For her part, when the little girl lives and assumes the tragic and beneficial situation of castration, she accepts that she has not the same right as her mother, and hence she doubly accepts that she has not the same right (phallus) as her father, since her mother has not this right (no phallus), although she is a woman, because she is a woman, and she simultaneously accepts that she has not the same right as her mother, i.e. that she is not yet a woman as her mother is. But she thereby gains in return her own small right: the right of a little girl, and the promise of a large right, the full right of a woman when she grows up, if she will grow up accepting the Law of Human Order, i.e. submitting to it if need be to deflect it – by not minding her p's and q's 'properly'.

In either case, whether it be the moment of dual fascination of the Imaginary (1) or the (Oedipal) moment of the lived recognition of the insertion into the Symbolic Order (2), the whole dialectic of the transition in all its essential details is stamped by the seal of Human Order, of the Symbolic, for which linguistics provides us with the *formal* laws, i.e. the *formal* concept.

Psycho-analytic theory can thus give us what makes each science no pure speculation but a science: the definition of the *formal* essence of its object, the precondition for any practical, technical application of it to its *concrete* objects. Thereby psycho-analytic theory escapes the classical idealist antinomies formulated by Politzer for example, when, while demanding of psycho-analysis (whose revolutionary theoretical scope he was the first in France to realize) that it be a science of the true 'concrete', a 'concrete psychology', he attacked it for its *abstractions*: the unconscious, the Oedipus complex, the castration complex, etc. How, said Politzer, can psycho-analysis claim to be the science of the *concrete* it aims to be and could be, if it persists in *abstractions* which are merely the 'concrete' alienated in an abstract and metaphysical psychology? How can one reach the 'concrete' from such abstractions, from the abstract? In fact, no science can do without abstraction, even when, in its 'practice' (which is not, NB, the theoretical practice of that science but the practice of its concrete *application*), it deals only with those peculiar and unique variants that constitute each individual 'drama'. As Lacan thinks them in Freud – and Lacan thinks nothing but Freud's concepts, giving them the form of our scientificity, the only scientificity there can be – the 'abstractions' of psycho-analysis are really the authentic scientific concepts of their object, insofar as, as concepts of their object, they contain within them the index, measure and basis for the necessity of their abstraction, i.e., the measure of their relation to the 'concrete', and hence of their specific relation to the concrete of their application, commonly called analytic practice (the cure).

So the Oedipal phase is not a hidden '*meaning*' which merely lacks consciousness or speech – it is not a structure buried in the past that can always be restructured or surpassed by 'reactivating its meaning'; the Oedipus complex is the dramatic structure, the 'theatrical machine'[7] imposed by the Law of Culture on every involuntary, conscripted candidate to humanity, a structure containing in itself not only the possibility of, but the necessity for the concrete variants in which it *exists*, for every individual who reaches its threshold, lives through it and survives it. In its application, in what is called its practice (the cure), psychoanalysis works on the concrete 'effects'[8] of these variants, i.e. on the modality of the specific and absolutely unique nexus in which the Oedipal transition was and is begun, completed, missed or eluded by some particular individual. These *variants* can be thought and known in their essence itself on the basis of the structure of the Oedipal *invariant*, precisely because this whole transition is marked from its beginnings in fascination, in its most 'aberrant' as well as in its most 'normal' forms, by the Law of this structure, the ultimate form of access to the Symbolic within the Law of the Symbolic itself.

I know that these brief suggestions will not only appear to be, but are, summary and schematic; that a number of notions put forward here require extended development if they are to be justified and established. Even if their well-foundedness and the relations they bear to the set of notions that underly them were clarified, even if they were compared with the letter of Freud's analyses, they would pose their own problems in their turn: not only problems of

7. An expression of Lacan's (*'machine'*), referring to Freud (*'ein anderes Schauspiel'* . . . *'Schauplatz'*). From Politzer, who talks of 'drama' to Freud and Lacan who speak of theatre, stage, *mise en scène*, machinery, theatrical genre, *metteur en scène*, etc., there is all the distance between the spectator who takes himself for the theatre – and the theatre itself.

8. If this term 'effect' is examined in the context of a classical theory of causality, it reveals a conception of the continuing presence of the cause in its effects (cf. Spinoza).

conceptual formation, definition and clarification, but real, new problems, necessarily produced by the development of the work of theorization we have just discussed. For example, how can we rigorously formulate the relation between the *formal* structure of language, the absolute precondition for the existence and intelligibility of the unconscious, on the one hand, the concrete kinship structures on the other, and finally the concrete ideological formations in which the specific functions implied by the kinship structures (paternity, maternity, childhood) are lived? Is it conceivable that the historical variation of these latter structures (kinship, ideology) might materially affect some or other aspect of the instances isolated by Freud? Or again, to what extent may the simple definition of the object and location of Freud's discovery, rationally conceived, react on the disciplines from which it distinguished itself (such as psychology, social psychology, sociology), and raise for them questions as to the (often problematic) status of their objects? And selecting one more from among so many possible questions: what relations are there between analytic theory and 1. the historical preconditions of its appearance, and 2. the social preconditions of its application?

1. *Who*, then, *was Freud, simultaneously* the founder of analytic theory and the inaugurator, as Analyst number one, *self-analysed*, original Father, of the long line of practitioners who claim descent from him?

2. *Who*, then, *are the psycho-analysts*, who *simultaneously* (and as naturally as if it went without saying) accept Freudian theory, the didactic tradition that descends from Freud, and the social and economic conditions (the social status of their 'associations' which cling tightly to the status of *medical* corporations) under which they practice? To what extent do the historical origins and socio-economic con-

ditions of the practice of psycho-analysis react an analytical theory and technique? Most important of all, to what extent do the theoretical *silence* of psychoanalysts about these questions (for this is certainly the state of affairs) and the theoretical *repression* these problems meet with in the world of analysis, affect both analytic theory and analytical technique in their content itself? Cannot the eternal question of the 'end of analysis', among others, be related to this repression, i.e. to the *non-thoughtness of these problems* which derive from an epistemological history of psycho-analysis and a social (and ideological) history of the world of analysis?

Here are a number of real questions, really posed, and they constitute immediately an equal number of fields of research. It may be that in the near future certain notions will emerge transformed from this test.

And this test is rooted in the test Freud, in his own field, applied to a particular legal, ethical and philosophical, i.e. definitively ideological, image of 'man', of the human 'subject'. Not in vain did Freud somtiemes compare the critical reception of his discovery with the upheavals of the Copernican Revolution. Since Copernicus, we have known that the earth is not the 'centre' of the universe. Since Marx, we have known that the human subject, the economic, political or philosophical ego is not the 'centre' of history – and even, in opposition to the Philosophers of the Enlightenment and to Hegel, that history has no 'centre' but possesses a structure which has no necessary 'centre' except in ideological misrecognition. In turn, Freud has discovered for us that the real subject, the individual in his unique essence, has not the form of an ego, centred on the 'ego', on 'consciousness' or on 'existence' – whether this is the existence of the for-itself, of the body-proper or of 'behaviour' – that the human subject is de-centred, constituted by a structure which has no 'centre' either, except in the imaginary misrecognition of the 'ego', i.e. in the ideological formations in which it 'recognizes' itself.

It must be clear that this has opened up one of the ways which may perhaps lead us some day to a better understanding of this *structure of misrecognition*, which is of particular concern for all investigations into ideology.

January 1964 (corrected February 1969)

BIBLIOGRAPHICAL STUDY NOTE:

Access to Lacan's work will be facilitated if it is approached in the following order:

1. 'Les complexes familiaux en pathologie', *Encyclopédie Française*, de Monzie, Vol. 8: 'La vie mentale' (1938).

2. 'La causalité psychique', *Évolution Psychiatrique*, fasc. 1, 1947.

3. 'Le stade du miroir comme formateur de la fonction du Je', *Écrits*, Paris 1966, pp. 93–100 (English translation, *New Left Review* 51, Sept.–Oct. 1968).

4. 'La chose freudienne', *Écrits*, pp. 401–36.

5. 'Les formations de l'inconscient', Seminar 1958–59. *Bulletin de psychologie*.

6. 'Les relations d'objet et les structures freudiennes', Seminar 1956–57, *Bulletin de psychologie*, 10.

7. 'Le désir et son interprétation', Seminar 1958–59, *Bulletin de psychologie*, Jan. 1960.

8. 'Fonction et champ de la parole et du langage en psychanalyse', *Écrits*, pp. 237–322 (English translation with a commentary by Anthony Wilden as *The Language of the Self*, Johns Hopkins Press, Baltimore, 1968). 'Remarque sur le rapport de Daniel Lagache: "Psychanalyse et structure de la personalite" ', *Écrits*, pp. 647–84; 'La direction de la cure et les principes de son pouvoir', *Écrits*, pp. 585–646; 'L'instance de la lettre dans l'inconscient ou la raison depuis Freud', *Ecrits*, pp. 493–528 (English translation, *Yale French Studies* 36–7, 1966, pp. 112–47); and other studies from the seven issues of the magazine *La Psychanalyse*.

9. Of texts written by Lacan's pupils or under his influence, the reader is advised to start with Serge Leclaire's articles in *La Psychanalyse*, Serge Leclaire and Jean Laplanche on the unconscious in *Les Temps Modernes*, July 1961, J. B. Lefèvre-Pontalis, 'Freud Aujourd'hui', *Les Temps Modernes*, 124–6 (1965), J. Laplanche's book on Hölderlin and Maud Mannoni: *L'enfant arriéré et sa mère*, 1963.

A Letter on Art
in Reply to André Daspre

La Nouvelle Critique has sent me your letter.[1] I hope you will permit me, if not to reply to all the questions it poses, at least to add a few comments to yours in the line of your own reflections.

First of all, you should know that I am perfectly conscious of the *very schematic* character of my article on Humanism.[2] As you have noticed, it has the disadvantage that it gives a 'broad' idea of ideology without going into the analysis of details. As it does not mention art, I realize that it is possible to wonder whether art should or should not be ranked as such among ideologies, to be precise, whether art and ideology are one and the same thing. That, I feel, is how you have been tempted to *interpret* my silence.

The problem of the relations between art and ideology is a very complicated and difficult one. However, I can tell you in what directions our investigations tend. *I do not rank real art among the ideologies*, although art does have a quite particular and specific relationship with ideology. If you would like some idea of the initial elements of this thesis and the very complicated developments it promises,

1. See *La Nouvelle Critique*, no. 175, April 1966, pp. 136–41.
2. *La Nouvelle Critique*, no. 164, March 1965; *For Marx*, pp. 242–7.

I advise you to read carefully the article Pierre Macherey
has written on 'Lenin as a critic of Tolstoy' in *La Pensée*,
No. 121, 1965.[3] Of course, that article is only a beginning,
but it does pose the problem of the relations between art
and ideology and of the specificity of art. This is the direction in which we are working, and we hope to publish
important studies on this subject in a few months time.

The article will also give you a first idea of the relationship between art and knowledge. Art (I mean authentic art,
not works of an average or mediocre level) does not give us a
knowledge in the *strict sense*, it therefore does not replace
knowledge (in the modern sense: scentific knowledge), but
what it gives us does nevertheless maintain a certain *specific
relationship* with knowledge. This relationship is not one of
identity but one of difference. Let me explain. I believe
that the peculiarity of art is to 'make us see' (*nous donner à
voir*), 'make us perceive', 'make us feel' something which
alludes to reality. If we take the case of the novel, Balzac or
Solzhenitsyn, as you refer to them, they make us *see*,
perceive (but not *know*) something which *alludes* to reality.

It is essential to take the words which make up this first
provisional definition literally if we are to avoid lapsing
into an identification of what art gives us and what science
gives us. What art makes us *see*, and therefore gives to us in
the form of '*seeing*', '*perceiving*' and '*feeling*' (which is not
the form of *knowing*), is the *ideology* from which it is born,
in which it bathes, from which it detaches itself as art, and
to which it *alludes*. Macherey has shown this very clearly
in the case of Tolstoy, by extending Lenin's analyses.
Balzac and Solzhenitsyn give us a 'view' of the ideology to
which their work alludes and with which it is constantly fed,
a view which presupposes a *retreat*, an *internal distantiation*

3. Now in Pierre Macherey, *Pour une théorie de la production littéraire*,
Paris, 1966, pp. 125–57.

from the very ideology from which their novels emerged. They make us 'perceive' (but not know) in some sense *from the inside*, by an *internal distance*, the very ideology in which they are held.

These distinctions, which are not just shades of meaning but specific differences, should *in principle* enable us to resolve a number of problems.

First the problem of the 'relations' between art and science. Neither Balzac nor Solzhenitsyn gives us any *knowledge* of the world they describe, they only make us 'see', 'perceive' or 'feel' the reality of the ideology of that world. When we speak of ideology we should know that ideology slides into all human activity, that it is identical with the 'lived' experience of human existence itself: that is why the form in which we are 'made to see' ideology in great novels has as its content the 'lived' experience of individuals. This 'lived' experience is not a *given*, given by a pure 'reality', but the spontaneous 'lived experience' of ideology in its peculiar relationship to the real. This is an important comment, for it enables us to understand that art does not deal with a reality *peculiar to itself*, with a *peculiar domain* of reality in which it has a monopoly (as you tend to imply when you write that 'with art, knowledge becomes human', that the object of art is 'the individual'), whereas science deals with a *different domain* of reality (say, in opposition to 'lived experience' and the 'individual', the abstraction of structures). Ideology is also an object of science, the 'lived experience' is also an object of science, the 'individual' is also an object of science. The real difference between art and science lies in the *specific form* in which they give us the same object in quite different ways: art in the form of 'seeing' and 'perceiving' or 'feeling', science in the form of *knowledge* (in the strict sense, by concepts).

The same thing can be said in other terms. If Solzhenitsyn does 'make us see' the 'lived experience' (in the sense defined earlier) of the 'cult of personality' and its effects, in no way does he give us a *knowledge* of them: this knowledge is the conceptual knowledge of the complex mechanisms which eventually produce the 'lived experience' that Solzhenitsyn's novel discusses. If I wanted to use Spinoza's language again here, I could say that art makes us 'see' 'conclusions without premises', whereas knowledge makes us penetrate into the mechanism which produces the 'conclusions' out of the 'premises'. This is an important distinction, for it enables us to understand that a novel on the 'cult', however profound, may draw attention to its 'lived' effects, but *cannot give an understanding of it*; it may put the question of the 'cult' on the agenda, but it cannot *define the means* which will make it possible to remedy these effects.

In the same way, these few elementary principles perhaps enable us to point the direction from which we can hope for an answer to another question you pose: how is it that Balzac, despite his personal political options, 'makes us see' the 'lived experience' of capitalist society in a critical form? I dó not believe one can say, as you do, that he *'was forced by the logic of his art to abandon certain of his political conceptions in his work as a novelist'*. On the contrary, we know that Balzac *never abandoned* his political positions. We know even more: his peculiar, reactionary political positions played a decisive part in the production of the content of his work. This is certainly a paradox, but it is the case, and history provides us with a number of examples to which Marx drew our attention (on Balzac, I refer you to the article by R. Fayolle in the special 1965 number of *Europe*). These are examples of a deformation of sense very commonly found in the dialectic of ideologies. See what Lenin says about Tolstoy (cf. Macherey's article): Tolstoy's personal ideological position is one component of the deep-lying causes of the *content* of his work. The fact that the content of the work of Balzac and Tolstoy is 'detached' from their political ideology and in some way makes us 'see' it from the *outside*, makes us 'perceive' it by a distantiation inside that ideology, *presupposes that ideology itself*. It is certainly possible to say that it is an 'effect' of *their art* as novelists that it produces this distance inside their ideology, which makes us 'perceive' it, but it is not possible to say, as you do, that art *'has its own logic'* which *'made Balzac abandon his political conceptions'*. On the contrary, *only because he retained them could he produce his work*, only because he stuck to his political ideology could he produce *in it* this internal 'distance' which gives us a critical 'view' of it.

As you see, in order to answer most of the questions posed for us by the existence and specific nature of art, we are forced to produce an adequate (scientific) *knowledge* of the processes which produce the 'aesthetic effect' of a work of art. In other words, in order to answer the question of the relationship between art and knowledge we must produce a *knowledge of art*.

You are conscious of this necessity. But you ought also to know that in this issue we still have a long way to go. The *recognition* (even the political recognition) of the existence and importance of art does not constitute *a knowledge of art*. I do not even think that it is possible to take as the beginnings of knowledge the texts you refer to,[4] or even Joliot-Curie, quoted by Marcenac.[5] To say a few words about the sentence attributed to Joliot-Curie, it contains a terminology

4. [Jean Marcenac, Elsa Triolet, Lukács, among others.
5. [Jean Marcenac, *Les Lettres Françaises*, 1966. 'I have always regretted the fact that F. Joliot-Curie never pursued the project he suggested to me at the time of Eluard's death, the project of a comparative study of poetic creation and scientific creation, which he thought might eventually prove an identity in their procedures.']

– 'aesthetic *creation*, scientific *creation*' – a terminology which is certainly quite common, but one which in my opinion must be *abandoned* and replaced by another, in order to be able to pose the problem of the knowledge of art in the proper way. I know that the artist, and the art lover, *spontaneously* express themselves in terms of 'creation', etc. It is a 'spontaneous' language, but we know from Marx and Lenin that every 'spontaneous' language is an *ideological* language, the vehicle of an ideology, here the ideology of art and of the activity productive of aesthetic effects. Like all knowledge, the knowledge of art presupposes a preliminary *rupture* with the language of *ideological spontaneity* and the constitution of a body of scientific concepts to replace it. It is essential to be conscious of the necessity for this rupture with ideology to be able to undertake the constitution of the edifice of a knowledge of art.

Here perhaps, is where I must express a sharp reservation about what you say. I am not perhaps speaking about exactly what you *want* or *would like* to say, but about what you *actually* do say. When you counterpose '*rigorous reflection on the concepts of Marxism*' to '*something else*', in particular to what art gives us, I believe you are establishing a comparison which is either incomplete or illegitimate. Since art in fact provides us with *something else* other than science, there is not an opposition between them, but a difference. On the contrary, if it is a matter of *knowing* art, it is absolutely essential to begin with '*rigorous reflection on the basic concepts of Marxism*': there is no other way. And when I say, '*it is essential to begin . . .*', it is not enough to *say* it, it is essential to *do* it. If not, it is easy to extricate oneself with a passing acknowledgement, like '*Althusser proposes to return to a rigorous study of Marxist theory. I agree that this is indispensable. But I do not believe that it is enough.*' My response to this is the only real criticism: there is a way of declaring an exigency 'indispensable' which consists precisely of *dispensing with it*, dispensing with a careful consideration of all its implications and consequences – by the acknowledgement accorded it in order to move quickly on to 'something else'. Now I believe that the only way we can hope to reach a real knowledge of art, to go deeper into the specificity of the work of art, to know the mechanisms which produce the 'aesthetic effect', is precisely to spend a long time and pay the greatest attention to the *'basic principles of Marxism'* and not to be in a hurry to 'move on to something else', for if we move on too quickly to 'something else' we shall arrive not at a *knowledge* of art, but at an *ideology* of art: e.g., at the latent humanist ideology which may be induced by what you say about the relations between art and the 'human', and about artistic 'creation', etc.

If we must turn (and this demands slow and arduous work) to the 'basic principles of Marxism' in order to be able to pose correctly, in concepts which are not the *ideological* concepts of aesthetic spontaneity, but *scientific* concepts adequate to their object, and thus necessarily *new* concepts, it is not in order to pass art silently by or to sacrifice it to science: it is quite simply in order to *know* it, and to give it its due.

April 1966

Cremonini, Painter of the Abstract

As I was standing in the hall at the Venice Biennale in which Cremonini[1] had exhibited some fine canvases, two Frenchmen came in, glanced quickly round and left, one saying to the other, 'Uninteresting: expressionism!' Since then, I have had occasion to read the same words from the pen of art criticism. Applied to Cremonini, the term 'expressionism' is a striking indication of a misunderstanding. All in all, it is the misunderstanding of all critical (and therefore of all aesthetic) judgement, which is no more than a commentary, at best a theoretical commentary, on aesthetic *consumption*: the ruling misunderstanding in contemporary art criticism, which, when it does not dress up its 'judgements' in the esotericism of a vocabulary communicating no more than the complicity of accomplices in ignorance, but consents to speak a plain language, reveals to one and all that it is no more than a branch of taste, i.e. of gastronomy.

1. Leonardo Cremonini was born at Bologna in 1925. He studied at the Academy of Fine Arts in Bologna and at the Brera Academy in Milan. Since 1951, the date of his first one-man exhibition at the Centre d'Art Italien, he has divided his time between Paris and long stays at Forio d'Ischia, Douarnenez, Panarea, Palermo, Forli, or in Spain. He has participated in exhibitions at the Tate Gallery, at the Biennales of San Marino and Venice, at the Rome Quadriennale, at the Paris Musée d'Art Moderne, as well as in Pittsburgh, New York, Beverly Hills and the Galerie du Dragon, Paris.

In order to 'see' Cremonini, and above all to talk about what he makes visible, we have to abandon the categories of the aesthetics of consumption: the gaze we need is different from that of desire for or disgust with 'objects'. Indeed, his whole strength as a figurative painter lies in the fact that he does not 'paint' 'objects' (those dismembered sheep; those tortured carcases; that stone; those plants; that 1900 armchair), nor 'places' (the sea, seen from the heavy articulated skeleton of an island; seen from a window open to the air; that balcony hanging in the sky; those rooms with polished wardrobes and beds; that dubious washroom; that compartment on a night train), nor 'times' or 'moments' (the morning at dawn; the night, high noon in a courtyard drenched in sunshine where little girls play hop-scotch). Cremonini 'paints' the *relations* which bind the objects, places and times. Cremonini is a *painter of abstraction*. Not an abstract painter, 'painting' an absent, pure possibility in a new form and matter, but a painter of the real *abstract*, 'painting' in a sense we have to define, real relations (as relations they are necessarily *abstract*) between 'men' and their 'things', or rather, to give the term its stronger sense, between 'things' and *their* 'men'.

To 'see' these relations in Cremonini's canvases is simultaneously to enter into other relations: those that obtain between the 'artist' and his 'work', or rather between the work and *its* artist. Here too, modern art criticism too often thinks these relations in the mysteries of the subjectivity of the painter, who inscribes his 'creative project' in the ideal materiality of his 'creation'. The aesthetics of consumption and the aesthetics of creation are merely one and the same: they both depend on the same basic ideological categories: (1) the category of the *subject*, whether creator or consumer (producer of a 'work', producer of an aesthetic judgement), endowed with the attributes of subjectivity (freedom, project, act of creation and judgement; aesthetic need, etc.); (2) the category of the *object* (the 'objects' represented, depicted in the work, the work as a produced or consumed object). Thus the subjectivity of creation is no more than the mirror reflection (and this reflection is aesthetic *ideology* itself) of the subjectivity of consumption: the 'work' is no more than the phenomenon of the artist's subjectivity, whether this subjectivity is psychological or transcendental-aesthetic. Cremonini leads us to the idea that the 'mystery' of the 'inwardness' of a painter, of his 'creative project', is no more than his work itself, that the relations between a painter and his 'work' are nothing but the 'relations' he 'paints'. Cremonini makes us see the relations between things and their men. At the same time, he makes us see, not the relations between the painter and his work, which have no *aesthetic* existence, but the relations between a 'work' and *its* painter, which are at the same time the relations between that work *and us*.

The individual *history* of Cremonini's painting is simply a commentary on this necessity: a refutation of the pure subjectivity of production, the mirror-reflection of the subjectivity of consumption.

This history is interesting not because it *began with* one 'object' and went on to another, but because of the *problems* confronted, which this history progressively and tenaciously poses, transforms and resolves.

In fact, Cremonini 'began' (one must 'begin' somewhere) with the *geological*: the armatures and articulations, consolidated by weight and history, of the passive body of an island, dormant in the heavy oblivion of the rocks, at the edge of an empty sea, a matter-less horizon. But he is already quite the opposite of a painter of 'objects', a landscape painter. All that he 'paints' about the rocks is what they ignore: their weight and memory (oblivion), i.e. their *difference* from something other than themselves, from what makes them the *ground* for men.

Cremonini went on to the *vegetable*: the sharp growth of a bulb, the long shriek of the dumb stems, the strident out-pouring of a flower displayed in the air like a bird of silence. He never 'painted' anything but the absences in these presences: the rhythm, the spurt, the snap of *time* 'depicted' by instantaneous, i.e. eternal, plants – and the cry of a voice, 'depicted' by something quite different, by gestures, trajectories and suspensions. Cremonini's next step was to *animals*: motionless sheep whose bones pierce their skin and snap in the paralysis of movement; flocks resembling the rock piles on which they graze; dogs frozen in a bronze rut; dismembered animals scattered among men collecting bony carcases, men like the carcases they bear on their emaciated shoulders. All that he 'painted' about the animals were the articulated bones, tailored in the very material of the rocks: articulations of the very living-ness of life, but frozen in death – and the few men he stiffened into the same material. The animals and *their* men, equally living corpses, circumscribed by the stone that they are, and by the air in which they think themselves free. What did Cremonini 'paint'? Similarities (rocks, bones, animals, men) where there are *differences* – and by 'painting' these similarities, he 'painted' differences: his animals and men are *distanced* from the nature fixed for them by our 'idea', i.e. by the ruling ideology, of man.

In conclusion, Cremonini came to the 'men' who had already prowled among the animals.

In his *individual* history as a painter, he had traversed and reproduced the whole cycle of a History (rocks, plants, animals, men), but in doing so he had showed that every god, even a painter-god, was absent, banished from it. He had reproduced this History in its material – or should we say 'materialist'? – order: the earth, plants, creatures, finally man. It is obvious that a certain ideology of the immediate relationship between man and nature provided the inspiration for Cremonini's work from the outset: what still fascinates him individually in the arm of a chair or in a tool is the fact that they extend the joints of the bony limbs of men and animals, and that these joints are no more than further patterns of nature related to the original patterns which made up the relationships of equilibrium and dis-equilibrium of the weight levers in his rocks. Hence the meaning that he could find in the *order* in which he had reproduced this History while living *his own* history: it could be the order of a *Genesis* (even a materialist one), i.e. of a *descent* from an origin containing the *true* meaning of things, the true relationship between man and nature, and his 'objects', above all the exemplary relationship between the craftsman and his material, his tools and his product.

It is highly probable that this ideological 'project' is what inspired, i.e. haunted Cremonini, and that the illusion it contained was part of the disposition of the means which ultimately produced his canvases and their peculiar history: the *result* (that is all that exists for us: the canvases that we are discussing) is precisely something *quite different* from this 'ideological' project. And the comparisons (the similarities) between the *forms* of the four orders (geological, vegetable, animal, human) are not *in fact* the canvases' *dominant* organizational principle: these comparisons are themselves subject to another organizational principle: that of the *differences*. At a certain moment, Cremonini might have *thought* he was painting only 'similarities', i.e. the 'isomorphisms' required to elaborate his ideological 'project' of the descent of forms (rocks, plants, articulated skeletons, tools, gestures . . .): *in fact*, these similarities were very soon subjected to a quite different logic: the logic of the *differences* which Cremonini has constantly 'painted', and foremost among them, the *difference from this ideological project of the descent of forms*. All this can be clearly 'seen' in the last stage of Cremonini's painting: the 'men'.

The men: they originally had, and still have, the *form* of their 'things', of 'things'. Bodies and faces of stone, revealing in their objects and gestures their primordial 'origins': precisely those bones transposed into tools, those thin elbows articulated into the arms of chairs, those women erect like the iron balustrades of their balconies, and their diminutive children. The men: beings congealed in their essence, in their past, in their origin, i.e. in their absence, which makes them what they are, never having asked to live, or why they should. The 'things': those tools, those utensils, walls, partitions separating the inside from the outside, the shade from the air, the sombre sheen of worn varnish from the harsh limpidity of the sky. The 'men': fashioned from the material of their objects, circumscribed by it, caught and defined once and for all: faces corroded by the air, gnawed and seemingly amputated (almost *too much* faces), gestures and cries congealed into immutable weight, a parody of human time reduced to eternity, the eternity of matter.

Then, only a few years ago, what spoke, silently, in this History began to appear: the *relations* between the men. It is not accidental that for Cremonini this object took the form of an exploration of *mirrors*, above all of the old mirrors of ordinary homes, the mirrors of shabby 1900 wardrobes: men at grips with their only wealth, the wretched past in which they *look at themselves*. They look at themselves: no, they *are* looked at. It is their mirrors, their wretchedness which fastens them, restoring to them despite themselves, whatever they do, their only inalienable possession: their own image.

Those women at the dressing-table do not see *themselves*

though they look at themselves in the mirror, even that young woman does not see *herself*, though *we* see her naked desire *on the back* of the looking-glass she holds in her hand: it is their mirrors that see them, and see the circle of their sight, though their mirrors are blind. The mirrors see the men, even in sleep and love: the implacable reflection, indifferent to its model, sees for us those beings of flesh, sleep, desire and waking, even in the hanging sky of their vertigo. However, in all these canvases, there are *tall vertical lines*: doors, windows, partitions, walls, in which is 'painted' the pitiless law which governs the men, even in their exhausted flesh: the *weight* of matter, i.e. of their lives.

No one could argue that it is by chance that the great *verticals* of the partitions and walls emerged in Cremonini's work at the same time as he came to paint in their mirrors the inexorable *circle* which dominates the connexions between men, through the connexions between objects and their men. The circles of the mirrors 'depict' a quite different *reference* than that of the similarity of forms in an ideology of *descent*. The circles of the mirrors 'depict' the fact that the objects and their forms, though related among themselves, are only so related because they turn in the same circle, because they are subject to the same law, which now 'visibly' dominates the relations between the objects and their men.

Furthermore, this *circle* really is a circle: it is 'cyclical', it has lost any origin; but along with the origin, it also seems to have lost any 'determination in the last instance'. The men and their objects refer us to the objects and their men, and *vice versa*, endlessly. And yet, the meaning of this circle is fixed, *behind the scenes*, by its *difference*: this difference is nothing but the presence, *alongside* the circle, of the great *verticals* of weight, which 'depict' *something other than* the perpetual reference of human-individuals to object-individuals and *vice versa* to infinity, *something other than* this circle of *ideological* existence: the determination of this circle by its *difference*, by a different, *non-circular* structure, by a law of quite a different nature, a weight which is irreducible to any Genesis, and haunts all Cremonini's later canvases in its *determinate absence*.

In the latest works, the *physical* presence of the mirrors is no longer required in order to 'paint' the circle. It becomes directly the circle of the inside and the outside, the circle of the gazes and gestures caught in the circle of things: thus the interior of the neighbouring flat seen through a window, while the neighbours look at that other interior from where they are seen; thus the holy butchers confused with the gigantic open carcases of beef which they are ransacking (circle of man and animal), turning towards the window (circle of the inside and the outside) where prohibition has drawn a little girl who runs away even before she has looked at them (circle of wish and prohibition); thus the game 'without rules' of the children running around the furniture – without rules, because its rule is merely the law of closure of a closed space, the only body of their 'freedom'. In their 'finite' world which dominates them, Cremonini thus 'paints' (i.e. 'depicts' by the play of the similarities inscribed in the differences) the history of men as a history *marked*, as early as the first childhood games, and even in the anonymity of faces (of children, women and men), by the *abstraction* of their sites, spaces, objects, i.e. *'in the last instance'* by the *real abstraction* which determines and sums up these first abstractions: the relations which constitute their *living conditions*.

I do not mean – it would be *meaningless* – that it is possible to 'paint' 'living conditions', to paint social relations, to paint the relations of production or the forms of the class struggle in a given society.[2] But it is possible, through their objects, to 'paint' visible connexions that depict by their disposition, the *determinate absence* which governs them. The structure which controls the *concrete* existence of men, i.e. which *informs the lived ideology* of the relations between men and objects and between objects and men, this structure, *as a structure*, can never be depicted by its presence, *in person*, positively, in relief, but only by traces and effects, negatively, by indices of absence, *in intaglio* (*en creux*). This intaglio (*creux*), which 'depicts' a *determinate* absence, is very precisely inscribed in the pertinent *differences* which we have been discussing: in the fact that a painted object does not conform to its essence, is compared with an object other than itself; in the fact that the normal connexions (e.g., the connexions between men and objects) are inverted and dislocated (*décalées*); lastly, in the fact, summing up all the others, that Cremonini can never paint a *circle* without simultaneously painting *behind the scenes*, i.e. alongside and away from the circle, but at the same time as it, and near it, something which rejects its law and 'depicts' the effectivity of a *different* law, absent in person: the great *verticals*.

Lastly, the final effect of this necessity, of the effectivity of the *abstract relations* which are the absent object of Cremonini's painting: what happens to human *faces*. It is these distorted and sometimes apparently monstrous, if not deformed faces, that have evoked the cry of expressionism. Those who have raised this cry still hold to a humanist-religious ideology of the function of the human face in art, and at the same time to an idealist ideology of *ugliness* (the

2. In my opinion, this is Planchon's error in his staging of Molière's *George Dandin*, at least as I saw it at Avignon in July 1966: it is not possible to stage social classes *in person* in a text which only deals with certain of their 'structural effects'.

aesthetic of ugliness is the ideology of expressionism), which confuses *deformation* with *deformity*. The humanist-religious ideological function of the human face is to be the seat of the 'soul', of subjectivity, and therefore the visible proof of the existence of the human *subject* with all the ideological force of the concept of the *subject* (the centre from which the 'world' is organized, because the human subject is the centre of its world, as a perceiving subject, as an active 'creative' subject, as a free subject and hence as responsible for its objects and their meaning).

Given these ideological premisses, it is obvious that the human face can only be painted as an identifiable and therefore recognizable individuality (certain individualizing *features*), recognizable even in the variations of its *uniqueness* (certain feelings which 'express' the religious quality and function of this subject, the *centre* and source of its 'world'). The aesthetic of *deformity* (of ugliness) is not in principle a critique and cancellation of these humanist-ideological categories, but merely a variant of them. That is why Cremonini's human faces are not expressionist, for they are characterized not by deformity but by *deformation*: their deformation is merely a determinate absence of form, a 'depiction' of their anonymity, and it is this anonymity that constitutes the actual cancellation of the categories of the humanist ideology. Strictly speaking, the deformation to which Cremonini subjects his faces is a *determinate* deformation, in that it does not replace one identity with another on the same face, does not give the faces one *particular* 'expression' (of the soul, the subject) instead of *another*: it takes *all expression* away from them, and *with it*, the ideological function which that expression ensures in the complicities of the humanist ideology of art. If Cremonini's faces are *deformed*, it is because they do not have the *form* of *individuality*, i.e. of *subjectivity*, in which 'men' immediately recognize that man is the *subject*, the centre, the author, the 'creator' of his objects and his world. Cremonini's human faces are such that they cannot be *seen*, i.e. identified as bearers of the ideological function of the expression of *subjects*. That is why they are so 'badly' represented, hardly outlined, as if instead of being the authors of their gestures, they were merely their *trace*. They are haunted by an absence: a purely negative absence, that of the humanist function which is refused them, and which they refuse; and a positive, determinate absence, that of the *structure* of the world which determines them, which makes them the anonymous beings they are, the structural effects of the real relations which govern them. If these faces are 'inexpressive', since they have not been individualized in the ideological form of identifiable subjects, it is because they are not the expression of their 'souls', but the expression, if you like (but this term is inadequate, it would be better to say the *structural effect*) of an absence, visible in them, the absence of the structural relations which govern their world, their gestures and even their experience of freedom.

All of 'man' is certainly present in Cremonini's work, but precisely because *it is not there*, because its double (negative, positive) absence is its very existence. That is why his painting is profoundly anti-humanist, and materialist. That is why his painting denies the spectator the complicities of communion in the complacent breaking of the humanist bread, the complicity which confirms the spectator in his spontaneous ideology by depicting it in 'paint'. Lastly, that is why his painting itself prevents him from recognizing himself as a 'creator' and *rejoicing* in the pictures he paints: for these pictures are the refutation *in actu* of the ideology of creation, even in aesthetics. This dislocation prevents Cremonini from *repeating* himself, i.e. from rejoicing in this recognition, and he cannot repeat himself because his painting denies him this recognition. If he constantly *discovers* and therefore changes, it is not, as with others, for reasons of taste or to test his skill, but because of the very logic of what he has been doing *from the outset*, despite his starting point, and the 'ideological project' with which he began. That an individual can abstract himself from his painting to this extent, i.e. can reject in it all the advantages of the complacency of self-recognition, that painting can to this extent abstract from its *painter* (i.e. refuse to be his own ideological mirror, the reflection of an ideology of 'aesthetic creation') are facts profoundly linked to the *significance* of this painting. If Cremonini does 'paint' 'abstract' relations, if he is the painter of abstraction I have tried to define, he can only 'paint' this abstraction on condition that he is present in his painting in the form determined by the relations he paints: in the form of their *absence*, i.e. in particular, in the form of *his own absence*.

It is precisely this radical anti-humanism of Cremonini's work which gives him such a power over the 'men' that we are. We cannot 'recognize' ourselves (ideologically) in his pictures. And it is because we cannot 'recognize' ourselves in them that we can *know* ourselves in them, in the specific form provided by art, here, by painting. If all that Cremonini 'paints' about 'man' is his reality: the 'abstract' relations which constitute him in his being, which make even his individuality and freedom – it is because he also knows that every painted work is only painted to be seen, and to be seen by living 'concrete' men, capable of determining themselves practically, within objective limits, determined, in their freedom, by the very 'sight' of what they are. Cremonini thus follows the path which was opened up to men by the great revolutionary thinkers, theoreticians and politicians, the great materialist thinkers who understood that the freedom of men is not achieved by the complacency of its ideological *recognition*, but by *knowledge* of the laws of their slavery, and that the 'realization' of their concrete individuality is achieved by the analysis and mastery of the abstract relations which govern them. In his own way, at his own level, with his own means, and in the element, not of philosophy or science, but of painting, Cremonini has taken the same road. This painter of the abstract, like the great revolutionary philosophers and scientists, would not paint, and would not paint the 'abstraction' of their world, if he did not paint for *concrete* men, for the only existing men, for us.

Every work of art is born of a project both aesthetic and ideological. When it exists as a work of art it produces *as a work of art* (by the type of critique and knowledge it inaugurates with respect to the ideology it makes us see) an *ideological* effect. If, as Establet has correctly, but too briefly, noted in a recent article,[3] 'culture' is the ordinary name for the Marxist concept of the *ideological*, then the work of art, as an *aesthetic object*, is no more part of 'culture' than instruments of production (a locomotive) or scientific knowledges are part of 'culture'. But like every other object, including instruments of production and knowledges, or even the corpus of the sciences, a work of art can become an *element* of the *ideological*, i.e. it can be inserted into the system of relations which constitute the ideological, which reflects in an imaginary relationship the relations that 'men' (i.e. the members of social classes, in our class societies) maintain with the structural relations which constitute their 'conditions of existence'. Perhaps one might even suggest the following proposition, that as the specific function of the work of art is to make *visible* (*donner à voir*), by establishing

3. See Roger Establet, ' "Culture" et idéologie', *Démocratie Nouvelle*, no. 6, 1966.

a distance from it, the reality of the existing ideology (of any one of its forms), the work of art *cannot fail to exercise* a directly ideological effect, that it therefore maintains far closer relations with ideology that any other *object*, and that it is impossible to think the work of art, in its specifically aesthetic existence, without taking into account the privileged relation between it and ideology, i.e. *its direct and inevitable ideological effect.* Just as a great revolutionary philosopher, like a great revolutionary politician, takes into account in his own thought the historical *effects* of his adoption of a position, even within the rigorous and objective system of his own thought – so a great artist cannot fail to take into account in his work itself, in its disposition and internal economy, the ideological *effects* necessarily produced by its existence. Whether this assumption of responsibility is completely lucid or not is a *different* question. At any rate, we know that 'consciousness' is secondary, even when it *thinks*, in the principle of materialism, its derivatory and conditioned position.

August 1966

Index

absence and presence, 230, 234, 236-40

abstraction, 52, 75-8, 116, 212, 215, 230, 236, 240-1

accumulation, primitive, 87-8

action, reciprocal, of the superstructure on the base, 135-136

aesthetics, 166, 177, 229-31, 238-42

alienation, 20, 22, 95, 115, 120-122, 160, 163-5, 215

animal, 205-6, 208-9, 232-3

alliance, class, 140-1, 146

Althusser, Louis, 90n, 189, 226
For Marx, 134n; *Reading Capital*, 134n

antagonism 18, 21, 85, 183

anthropology, philosophical, 16, 121-2, 201-2, 206

Aquinas, St Thomas, 179

aristocracy, 152-3

Aristotle, 16, 42, 91, 166

army, 133, 137, 143, 148, 152-3, 156

art, 221-7, 229-42; history of, 72

autonomy, relative, of the superstructure, 135-6, 149

Aveling, Edward, 90

axiomatics, 41

Bachelard, Gaston, 29, 38

Balzac, Honoré de, 222-5

Barth, Karl, 163

Bazarov, Vladimir Alexandrovich, 25

behaviourism, 201-2

Beltov, *see* Plekhanov

Bergson, Henri, 28

Berkeley, George, 47, 51, 55

Bernheim, Hippolyte, 199

Binswanger, Ludwig, 202

biology, 25, 39, 190-2, 197, 202, 206, 211n, 212, 212n

birth, 176, 191, 195-6, 200, 211

Bismark, Prince Otto von, 153

Bogdanov, Alexander Alexandrovich, 25, 50, 57

Bolsheviks, (RSDRPb), 24-6, 29, 51, 69, 96, 109

bourgeoisie, 7-8, 17, 19, 85, 91, 100-1, 104, 128-9, 137, 152-3
dictatorship of, 139

Boutroux, Émile, 28

break, epistemological, 38-40, 41-2, 93, 101, 173, 195, 226

Breuer, Josef, 200

Brunschvicg, Léon, 28

Cabanis, Pierre Jean Georges, 158

capital, constant and variable, 96-7, 130n; organic composition, 92, 96-7, 103; total social, 75, 97

capitalism, 72-3, 82-8, 91, 98,

MONTHLY REVIEW

an independent socialist magazine
edited by Paul M. Sweezy and Harry Magdoff

Business Week: ". . . a brand of socialism that is thorough-going and tough-minded, drastic enough to provide the sharp break with the past that many left-wingers in the underdeveloped countries see as essential. At the same time they maintain a sturdy independence of both Moscow and Peking that appeals to neutralists. And their skill in manipulating the abstruse concepts of modern economics impresses would-be intellectuals. . . . Their analysis of the troubles of capitalism is just plausible enough to be disturbing."

Bertrand Russell: "Your journal has been of the greatest interest to me over a period of time. I am not a Marxist by any means as I have sought to show in critiques published in several books, but I recognize the power of much of your own analysis and where I disagree I find your journal valuable and of stimulating importance. I want to thank you for your work and to tell you of my appreciation of it."

The Wellesley Department of Economics: " . . . the leading Marxist intellectual (not Communist) economic journal published anywhere in the world, and is on our subscription list at the College library for good reasons."

Albert Einstein: "Clarity about the aims and problems of socialism is of greatest significance in our age of transition. . . . I consider the founding of this magazine to be an important public service." (In his article, "Why Socialism" in Vol. I, No. 1.)

DOMESTIC: $11 for one year, $20 for two years, $9 for one-year student subscription.

FOREIGN: $13 for one year, $23 for two years, $10 for one-year student subscription. (Subscription rates subject to change.)

62 West 14th Street, New York, New York 10011

Modern Reader Paperbacks